The Cognitive Challenge of War

The Cognitive Challenge of War

Prussia 1806

Peter Paret

PRINCETON UNIVERSITY PRESS

Princeton and Oxford

Copyright © 2009 by Princeton University Press

Published by Princeton University Press, 41 William Street,

Princeton, New Jersey 08540

In the United Kingdom: Princeton University Press,

6 Oxford Street, Woodstock, Oxfordshire OX20 1TW

Library of Congress Cataloging-in-Publication Data

Paret, Peter.

The cognitive challenge of war : Prussia, 1806 / Peter Paret.

p. cm.

Includes bibliographical references and index.

ISBN 978-0-691-13581-6 (hardcover : alk. paper)

1. Napoleonic Wars, 1800–1815—Campaigns—Germany—Prussia.

2. Jena, Battle of, Jena, Germany, 1806.

3. Auerstedt, Battle of, Auerstedt, Germany, 1806.

4. Napoleonic Wars, 1800–1815—Social aspects—Germany—Prussia.

5. Napoleonic Wars, 1800–1815—Art and the war.

6. Napoleonic Wars, 1800–1815—Literature and the war.

7. Clausewitz, Carl von, 1780–1831—Military leadership.

8. Jomini, Antoine Henri, baron de, 1779–1869—Military leadership.

9. Military history—Case studies.

10. Military art and science—Case studies.

I. Title.

DC229.P28 2009

940.2'742—dc22   2009020516

British Library Cataloging-in-Publication Data is available

This book has been composed in Bembo

Printed on acid-free paper. ∞

press.princeton.edu

Printed in the United States of America

1 3 5 7 9 10 8 6 4 2

Contents

Illustrations

MAPS

ILLUSTRATIONS

Acknowledgments

The Lees Knowles Lectures, a somewhat expanded text of which has been turned into this book, were given at the University of Cambridge in October and November 2008. In that time my wife and I were the guests of Trinity College, and I want to express our gratitude to the Master, Lord Rees, and the Fellows of Trinity for making our stay with them so agreeable and interesting. It was an exhilarating start of the day each morning to step out of the Master's Lodge into the Great Court, framed by the fronts of buildings in which fellows and students had lived and studied for centuries. I am indebted to friends and colleagues at two younger institutions, professors J. Lionel Gossman and Walter H. Hinderer of Princeton University and John W. Shy of the University of Michigan, each of whom gave me helpful comments and criticism from the perspective of his discipline, as well as to two anonymous readers for indicating their approbation of the manuscript—together with useful questions and suggestions—to Princeton University Press.

As so often before, it has been a pleasure to work with the editors of the Press—in particular Brigitta van Rheinberg, editor-in-chief and executive editor, history, who gave me her detailed comments and questions, Nathan Carr, Clara Platter, and Anita O'Brien, who copyedited the manuscript with a light touch.

The Cognitive Challenge of War

I

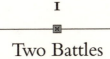

Two Battles

These pages discuss the response to innovation in war. "It is right to learn even from one's enemies," wrote Ovid. Right, but not necessarily easy. In exploring the issue, I shall address specifics much of the time, but to begin it might be useful to remind ourselves of some basic facts.

▣ I ▣

The components of war—mobilization of human resources, discipline, weapons, tactics, strategy, and much else, the issues they raise, and the problems they pose—are timeless. But the forms they take and the social context that does much to shape them are always changing. How people react to change and innovation in war, or fail to react, is as meaningful as are the changes themselves. Responses are of two kinds. One is the military's desire and ability—strong or feeble—to master innovation, whether in technology, doctrine, or policy. The response may be to specific issues—the introduction of the tank and of poison gas in the First World

War, the emergence or reemergence of the suicide bomber in our time—or to broad developments, in recent centuries, for instance, the Western world's growing reliance on conscription. The other response is that of society itself, the public's awareness of a new weapon or of one or the other belligerent's motives and methods that seem to reflect new ideas. Here the principal problem is not how to defeat or make use of innovation, but how to live with it. An example is the tolerance of modern societies to wars of long duration and to casualties that in a week may run into the thousands, as happened in the two world wars.

The two kinds of response bear on each other. The soldier's knowledge helps guide public opinion; social characteristics and attitudes influence the soldier's analysis. The importance of the military's response is obvious, but the response of society to new ideas or methods in war, driven less by analyses than by anxiety and assumptions based on class and culture, is also significant. It may influence immediate events, stimulate confidence or fear, and, as it blends with other tendencies, color more lasting attitudes and expectations. As much as the military's response, a society's reaction to its perception of the new in war affects subsequent policy and behavior.

To recognize innovation, whether in military institutions and how they function, or in their leaders and how they think, is itself a change. Even then society and soldiers will not find it easy to understand the new. Cultural preconceptions and institutional and individual self-interest may block understanding. Further cognitive barriers add to the difficulties. In any conflict, the enemy's stated or perceived aims, the likely consequences of defeat, affect reactions to the war. A third barrier, beyond the need to comprehend what may now be expected in war, and how a particular war may alter one's condition, is or may be the challenge of understanding war itself. To achieve it is not always necessary. A weapon or method can be countered even if one does not see beyond the immediate issue. Still, a broader understanding remains desirable. Above all, it is important to keep in mind that wars are fought not to be won but to gain an objective beyond war. War, however, is not only a complex social, organizational, technological, and political reality, its ambiguous character engages emotion as well as reason. Once combat begins and people die, it may be difficult to remember the instrumentality of war, and to realize that victory is not invariably followed by reward. Everything in war may have consequences beyond the operational or strategic intent. How often has success itself proved counterproductive—perhaps because of the manner in which it was achieved! War exists to implement policy, whether or not that policy is rational. But war also creates conditions and engenders feelings that may weigh on and interfere with its instrumentality. The employment of violence can be rational. And yet violence and its effects are always emotional and subject to the irrational—even when the violent act is justified, as it may be in self-defense. The emotional impact of violence on perpetrator and recipient never dissipates in a vacuum. When soldiers burn a village

The historical episode I want to address is the war of 1806 between France and Prussia and some of its consequences. A discussion of generalities in their historical context will find the Napoleonic wars a useful arena. They occurred at a time of great change in the organization and use of force. They have been much explored and are familiar even to nonspecialists. Among them, the war of 1806 has advantages and disadvantages for our purpose. Two systems of warfare clashed, and a conventional, time-tested way of raising troops, of training and fighting, was not only defeated but demolished. To be sure, the belligerents were not equal in military power and economic resources. The Prussian army had not seen action since the middle 1790s, after which the French army had become the strongest and most seasoned military force in the world. The French also began the war with a strategic advantage, the war of 1805 having ended with parts of the *Grande Armée* remaining deep in Germany. The outcome of such an uneven conflict may therefore prove little. But history is better at revealing than at proving, and states do not interact in controlled laboratory conditions that allow comparisons of precisely equal elements. We must study war in the shifting reality in which it occurs.

■ 2 ■

The conflicts between 1792 and 1815 mark stages in a system of mobilizing men and resources and of warfare that emerged in the revolution, to be further developed under Napoleon. In always different combinations of plans and execution, new elements interacted with institutions and methods retained from the ancien régime. By 1806, roughly halfway in this dense sequence of wars, the new system had matured and was not yet declining into the less supple, increasingly weary forms it assumed in the empire's later campaigns. Napoleon thought the army of 1806 the best he ever led.

Conditions on the other side were more complex. The Prussian army was no longer that of Frederick the Great. But despite many changes, its organization and doctrine remained basically those of his last years. Some officers serving against republican armies in the early 1790s recognized the need for adjustments. In 1795 a Military Reorganization Commission was established. But it dealt principally with the increase in territory and population resulting from the Third Partition of Poland, and the changes it instituted did little to improve the army's performance in 1806. Another change, this one certainly significant, was a step backward: the strategic and operational thinking of the men now in charge was less imaginative, more cautious, than it had been under Frederick, who tried to impart to his senior generals some of his own uncompromising understanding of the use of force. Under his very different heirs, the Prussian military were ill prepared to learn from, let alone accept, the republican armies' innovations in organization, command, and execution.

To soldiers wherever they served, the wars of the French Revolution and of Napoleon posed problems ranging from the methods of raising troops and the structure of military forces to ways of fighting. To their societies the technical challenge of the wars was less important than their psychological, social, and moral impact. Looking back from the 1820s, Clausewitz noted that these wars had moved from the eighteenth-century ideal of limited conflict between standing armies, which left the social and economic environment relatively untouched, toward a new concept of unlimited or "total" war. In one of the last chapters of *On War*, he wrote that after 1792 "war, untrammeled by any conventional restraints, . . . [broke] loose in all its elemental fury. . . . Will this always be the case in the future? From now on will every war in Europe be waged with the full resources of the state . . . ? Such questions are difficult to answer." Clausewitz concluded his statement by extending his definition of war as unalloyed violence into a historical and predictive dimension: "But the reader will agree with us when we say that once barriers—which in a sense consist only in man's ignorance of what is possible—are torn down, they are not so easily set up again."[1]

Before the revolution the separation of war from civilian life was far from absolute, but it was more protective—especially in its exclusion of the middle range of society from military service—than the later concept of total war, which was to receive its loudest welcome in totalitarian regimes but was embraced elsewhere as well. In the conflicts that began in 1792 and changed Europe's political organization and part of its social structure, contemporaries experienced the events of 1806 as a powerful illumination of the new way of war, perhaps even of a new Iron Age descending on Europe.[2]

I shall now outline the campaign of 1806, the methods of the French army, and the difficulties the Prussians experienced in countering them. The following chapters address responses to these events. This chapter provides the raw material, which the succeeding chapters convert into discussions of art and literary history, political history, and the history and analysis of theory. The second chapter shifts from campaign history to examine German reactions to 1806 in broadsheets and in the fine arts and literature, which signal the extension of war to all classes of society, an expansion that created a new environment for policy and theory. In a further shift, the third chapter addresses Prussian political and institutional responses to the defeats. Social and political change, military reform, paintings and popular prints, novels and dramas—all respond to the new, and all bear on each other. The final chapter takes up yet another perspective by examining the ideas of several theorists of war, in particular of two men, who fought on opposing sides in 1806, Jomini and Clausewitz. Their considered reactions to their experiences link the war of 1806 to two competing ways of thinking about war, which were to have a long life and continue to influence us today.

⊠ 3 ⊠

In 1795 Prussia withdrew from the War of the Second Coalition against France and for the next decade followed a policy of neutrality, claiming the role of protector of the north-German states, while extending her rule to the territories gained in the last two partitions of Poland. In the meantime French expansion in Italy, Germany, and the Low Countries continued. War resumed in Central Europe in 1803. Napoleon's hint that he might cede Hanover to Prussia induced Berlin not to join the new anti-French coalition. After occupying Vienna and defeating the Russians and Austrians at Austerlitz, parts of the French army took up quarters in southern Germany, and Prussia found herself not only politically but strategically isolated, a condition that a new secret agreement with Russia could not immediately lift (map 1). At last recognizing the danger, which even less clumsy diplomacy might not have avoided, Frederick William III ordered the partial mobilization of the Prussian army, called on his reluctant ally Saxony for assistance, and demanded the withdrawal of French forces from Germany. Napoleon replied by instructing his ambassador to leave Berlin unless Prussia demobilized. He ignored a new ultimatum, and on October 9, before Russian armies had come to her support, Prussia declared war, an ill-considered measure to forestall a French attack.

Prussia went to war to restore the status quo. Napoleon's intentions were more expansive. Victory would bring all of Germany under his control, extend his reach along the Baltic into Eastern Europe, deny Continental markets to the British economy, and mount a threat or draw a forward line of defense against Russia. His resources seemed adequate for the purpose. The population of France, to mention only this,

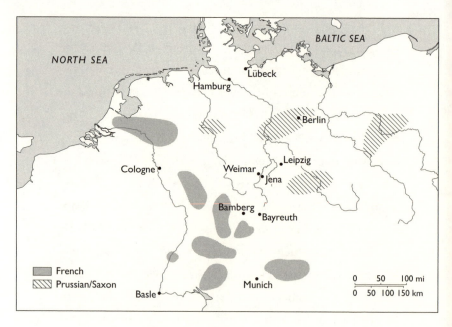

MAP I

French and Prussian Troop Concentrations, September 1806

was three times that of Prussia, as Napoleon pointed out in a taunting letter to Frederick William as the first shots were being exchanged.[3] Yet the first weeks of the war, which were also its decisive phase, did not reflect this disparity. Considering only the size of the opposing forces in October, a Prussian victory remained possible and might have blunted the French threat until Russian help arrived. But already at an early stage weaknesses became apparent, ranging from the strategic conceptions of the senior commanders to the army's organization and tactical methods, which were to hinder Prussian operations throughout the campaign.

Frederick the Great had put his trust in rapid offensives with concentrated force, even at the risk of leaving important targets unprotected, as he allowed Berlin to be raided by Austrian and Russian forces in the Seven Years War. Very different was another influential strategic system, which de-emphasized battle and instead stressed the art of controlling key points and of maneuvering the enemy into unfavorable positions, even at the cost of dividing one's forces. In 1806 the Prussian commander-in-chief, the Duke of Brunswick, did not discount the importance of physically defeating the enemy; but he could not free himself from seeing battle as a dangerous last resort, and as the king's presence with the army led to frequent councils of war, arguments in favor of caution and safety inevitably diluted more aggressive proposals—a problematical response to an opponent who expanded on Frederick's rapid deployment of concentrated force with larger armies and far more ambitious goals.

The organization of the Prussian army acted as a further brake. Above the regiment, its executive and administrative structure was adequate for maneuvers; in war it was stretched to the limit. Despite some last-minute reshuffling of the table of organization, regiments were not grouped in permanent brigades, in which they learned to act together. The senior staff officers of the field commanders had limited authority and differed in their operational concepts. The commander-in-chief's staff, small and further handicapped by a scarcity of maps, found it difficult to coordinate the various parts of the army. Disciplinary concerns and the prevailing moral code precluded soldiers from living off the land, which tied the army to a ponderous network of depots and supply trains and reduced mobility, the more so since, in contrast to the highly drilled rank and file, the wagoners and drovers were civilians. Nor was it helpful to burden the supply service with grooms and hay wagons for the horses infantry officers kept to ride or use as carriage horses on the march—one of several ways the privilege of rank slowed the army. In these matters the French were more consequential. When Napoleon issued operational orders to his marshals, he did not feel it beneath his dignity to warn against the presence of unauthorized horses.[4] Like their opponents, the French never had sufficient maps and suffered from the difficulty of coordinating widely separated units by means of messengers. Napoleon's constant demand that his generals keep him informed of their location did not prevent an entire corps from slipping out of his control during the campaign. But his strategic sense, operational intelligence, and energy made up for these and other flaws.

Prussian weaknesses in organization were amplified by a tactical system less versatile than that of the French. In itself that need not have been fatal. The high casualties the French were to suffer in 1806 suggest that Prussian tactics, however old-fashioned, might yet have succeeded had the army been organized in larger units, with a strong central command and better means of control and communication. But deficient tactics made success even less likely and turned defeat to disaster. Eighteenth-century war, whatever its formalities, had responded realistically to the society, political culture, and military technology of the time. As perfected under Frederick, Prussian tactics defeated opponents using basically similar methods. When changed political forces affected the conduct of war toward the end of the century, the Prussian system no longer worked as well.

French and Prussian tactics remained similar in some respects, yet in recent years they had developed significant differences. In both armies the infantry fought in linear formations. It required intense drill and discipline to open marching columns into the extended lines of two or three ranks that enabled large numbers of men to fire simultaneously or to deliver the irregular but continuous fire to which volleys degenerated in combat. Endless training was needed to change the direction of the line, or convert firing lines to bayonet charges or into battalion squares to repel cavalry. In the French army marching columns could also thicken into so-called battalion or attack columns, wider than deep, which brought large numbers of men quickly to the enemy—a formation in Prussia still rejected in favor of the more difficult method of advancing in line. Columns and lines could detach groups of skirmishers to cover their movement and to fight in woods, broken terrain, or villages. That was also done in Prussia, but rarely since it went against the assumption that only absolute trust in the linear system could fuse large numbers of men into the mobile cohesion that was its greatest strength. How was the same soldier to be taught the automatic responses demanded by linear tactics and the initiative required in skirmishing? The French army solved this problem by making do with less precision and slower volleys, and by relying on the ambition, good will, and patriotic commitment of the rank and file, turned by the revolution from subjects to citizens of that great abstraction, the nation. Prussian soldiers, in contrast, were still the product of regionally centered, corporative societies, the privileges and duties of each constituent group fixed by law and custom. Soldiers came from the least privileged segments of the population, mainly agricultural laborers tied to the land, or were foreigners serving for pay. The harsh discipline to which they were subject was not moderated when complexities of drill proliferated after Frederick the Great's death.

By 1800 the French had gone far to develop tactics that responded to the new possibilities the revolution created. Line and column were made more versatile by attaching a company of light infantry to each infantry regiment for skirmishing and scouting. But whether soldiers wore the uniforms of grenadiers, line infantry, or *voltigeurs,* all were expected to fight with reasonable competence in column, line, and open order. At the time some observers regarded French infantry tactics, especially skirmishing, as the decisive innovation of the new wars. In works soon translated into French and English, a German analyst, the former Prussian officer Heinrich Dietrich von Bülow, predicted that future battles would be fought by skirmishers.[5] Others saw the new tactics merely as one important change among many. For everyone they marked an obvious, factually and symbolically significant difference between the old and the new—between drilled mechanical obedience and the self-sufficient skirmisher and sniper.

The need to expand tactical possibilities did not go unnoticed in Prussia. Combinations of open and close order were tested, but it was decided to develop specialists instead: fusilier or light infantry battalions, drilled formalistically to break up the close formation and fight *en debandade* with a plethora of signals and commands, and one regiment of *chasseurs* or *Fussjäger*, an elite unit armed with rifles rather than muskets. Its men mostly came from a better order of society than did grenadiers or musketeers: from families of small landowners, foresters, minor officials. Drill and discipline were less harsh, and after retiring they could expect employment in the state administration. In an army dominated by tradition, the *Fussjäger* were a force for modernism; but the regiment also exemplified the army's segmented character, and its 1,500 men were never sufficient to confront "the new Gauls" in forests, hills, and villages where the line soon became helpless.

The cavalry matched the infantry's low level of integration. In peacetime it rarely trained in large formations; in war it was not, as in France, routinely committed in massive force once artillery fire and infantry volleys weakened the enemy line. Instead, regiments or even squadrons were frittered away in costly attacks. The artillery suffered similar disjunctions. Light guns were attached to each regiment, but their effectiveness was limited, and they slowed down the infantry. The heavy artillery was difficult to move and supply; much of it was not even mobilized in 1806. Only horse artillery could keep up in mobile operations. In the campaign that now began, Prussian commanders rarely matched their opponents' practice of massing artillery to support an advance or repel an attack. The two armies had similar social and political antecedents in early absolutism; but more recently, in response to the pressures and opportunities of the French Revolution, one had taken a new direction.

■ 4 ■

In early September Napoleon, believing that war was now likely, began preparations for a rapid, sharp campaign. From Saint-Cloud he sent Berthier, his chief of staff temporarily in command in Germany, instructions for readying the army, which was being reinforced from France, and for scouting the approaches to Prussia. At the beginning of the nineteenth century, the undulating, mostly open country north of the Thuringian Forest, well suited for the maneuver of large forces, was thinly populated. Jena had six thousand inhabitants; twelve miles to the west, Weimar, thanks to Goethe a center of European culture, less than eight thousand—small communities on which several hundred thousand French and German soldiers now descended.

The Duke of Brunswick assembled the Prussian army and its Saxon contingent south of Weimar and Jena, some 140 miles south of Berlin, their effective strength of 161,000 reduced by the many units on long-range reconnaissance or covering what were deemed key positions. Brunswick had three options: advance on the French now assembling in south-central Germany; attack them at Jena as they moved north; or withdraw to his Prussian base, and in this strong position stop them in a defensive battle—politically out of the question since it left Saxony open to the enemy. He decided to attack while the French army was still concentrating. This required a degree of speed his forces could not generate, and early in October, before he had gone far, the French began to move north (map 2). They advanced in three main columns, separated by one or two days' march: in the west the corps of Lannes and Augereau; in the center Bernadotte, Davout, the light and heavy cavalry, and Napoleon with the Guard; to the east Soult, Ney, and troops of the Confederation of the Rhine—together slightly over 160,000 men.[6] On paper this formation—the emperor famously compared it to a gigantic battalion square—appears simple; on the ground, maintaining the square's cohesion as it advanced, and assuring the mutual support of its parts against unpredictable enemy action, demanded experience, energetic supervision, and the instinctive search for battle.

Napoleon had only a vague idea of Brunswick's location and intentions. But in his mind he pictured an advance north that would place Berlin and Prussian communications to Russia in immediate danger. Threatening a move by a second, smaller force from the Rhine east would hint at the possibility of a two-pronged envelopment and afford some protection in the unlikely event Prussia could spare troops

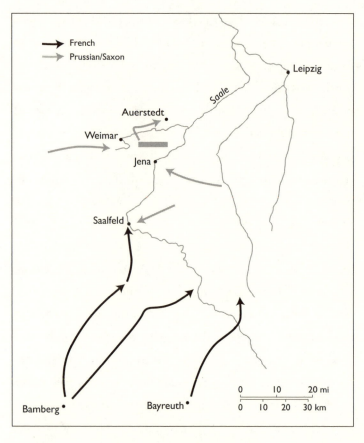

MAP 2
Operations up to October 10

to cut the *Grande Armée*'s lines of communication to France. The idea was as good as it was obvious. It was predicted by Jomini, Ney's chief of staff, and the Prussians expected it. The map showed Napoleon the importance of the Saale River flowing northwest to Saalfeld, where it bends sharply and runs north, past Jena and Magdeburg to the Elbe. From

Saalfeld he could proceed west or east of the river. On September 30, before joining the army, he ordered Berthier to prepare for a general advance, far enough east to outflank the enemy, and added: "I intend to arrive in Saalfeld before strong enemy forces reach it."[7] As he was writing, a Prussian advance guard of some 9,000 men under Prince Louis Ferdinand, a nephew of Frederick the Great and an unusually able, aggressive officer, was nearing the town, where on October 10 he came upon lead units of Lannes' corps.

When Brunswick learned that the chance to catch the French piecemeal was gone, he halted his advance. Bernadotte's pressure on his units farthest east prompted him to turn back toward Weimar and Jena. At Saalfeld, Louis Ferdinand, badly informed, believed he had to stand fast. Later rumors that he disobeyed orders to withdraw seem to have been false. Leading a cavalry attack to break through the French lines that threatened to encircle him, he was killed and his command was driven back with the loss of 1,700 men and 34 guns. The news of his defeat and death soon reached Jena and caused panic among some of the troops there, already suffering from the supply train's failure to keep up. Some Saxon units were left without rations for two days, and their officers began to talk of quitting their Prussian allies—administrative and disciplinary failures that were further signs of the brittleness of Brunswick's army.

By October 13 the western French column, continuing north from Saalfeld, was within sight of Jena, which Davout, eleven miles to the east, had already passed (map 3). The

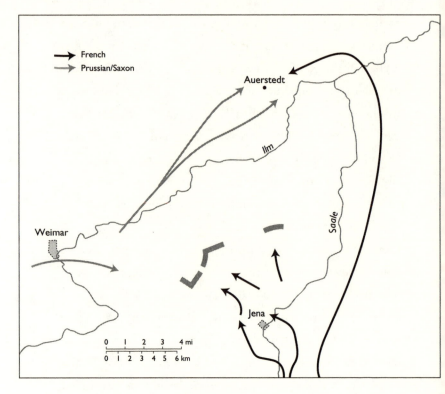

MAP 3
October 13–14

Prussians, about to be cut off from Magdeburg and Berlin, accelerated their retreat. Brunswick with the main army marched from Weimar toward Auerstedt. To guard its flank, a force under Prince Hohenlohe deployed 40,000 men on a plateau west of Jena, leaving some 15,000 under Rüchel to cover Weimar and act as reserve, too far back to support the main force quickly. At about the same time Napoleon ordered Lannes and Augereau to occupy Jena, cross the Saale,

CHAPTER I

20

and attack Hohenlohe's force, which he assumed to be the main Prussian army, while to the north Davout changed direction and turned southwest against the Prussian left flank. Depending on how far he had gone, Bernadotte was to support either Davout or the troops around Jena, where the emperor expected to fight. Whether from ill will or lassitude, or because he misunderstood his orders, Bernadotte did neither, and his 20,000 men had no part in the two battles fought within their hearing on the following day.

In the afternoon of the 13th, Napoleon rode through Jena, which here and there French units were already looting, to examine the terrain of the coming battle. From his study, Hegel, working on the last pages of his *Phenomenology of Spirit*, observed, as he wrote to a friend, "the emperor, this soul of the world, ride out of town. . . . Truly it is a remarkable sensation to see such an individual on horseback, raising his arm over the world and ruling it."[8] The odd term "soul of the world" (*Weltseele*) Hegel borrowed from the philosopher Schelling, who meant by it the force that integrates the world's organic and abstract elements, which seems far-fetched when applied to Napoleon. Possibly Hegel associated *Weltseele* with the concept of the "beautiful soul" in his *Phenomenology*, an autonomous force, acting as it must, in disregard of convention, tradition, and other peoples' interests—not a bad characterization of Napoleon, whom Hegel, in accord with his earlier enthusiasm for the reformist phase of the French Revolution, admired for his modernizing policies, not least in the empire's German satellites.

With the compound *Weltseele,* Hegel seems to identify the emperor as a life force raised to the highest power, a force that destroys but, Godlike, also creates.

At the edge of Jena, Napoleon gained only a vague impression of the plateau that rises above the town and extends some miles west. Parts were occupied by Prussian troops; but units of Lannes's corps already had a foothold on its edge. Napoleon ordered the rest of the corps and the Guard to move up the slopes after dark. Other French forces headed for Jena to add weight to the planned breakout from the bridgehead and support it with flanking operations north and south, some 55,600 men on the morning of the 14th, with another 40,300 expected by early afternoon—more than twice Hohenlohe's 40,000 men.

Before sunrise on the morning of the 14th, fog still on the ground, Napoleon gave the order to attack. Fighting began on the eastern end of the plateau, where Hohenlohe, who should have fought a rearguard action as the main army marched northeast, was drawn into a pitched battle. After three hours the Prussians had been cleared from the forward area of the plateau. The French could now spread out and advance against the Prussian second line of defense in the center and west of the plateau along the Weimar road, the link to the reserves a few miles away, which Hohenlohe had called forward at eight o'clock. Both sides developed their forces for the next major move, while groups of marksmen ranged ahead of the French lines, their preferred targets officers, whose braided hats, some with plumes, marked them out. The embellishment of uniforms at the expense of their former functional simplicity, as the intricacies added to Prussian tactics after Frederick the Great's death, were complexities characteristic of the last stage of a style, in war as in art. Against aimed fire distinctive dress for officers proved self-destructive. A village in the center of the Prussian line was taken by Lannes, lost again, and recaptured by Ney's lead units. Soon after ten o'clock Hohenlohe advanced his infantry, drums and fifes playing, and pushed the French back. Frederician doctrine now called for a bayonet attack; instead, the battalions halted by the village, probably to await the reserves from Weimar. But the reserves did not come. Perhaps Rüchel started late. That he needed five hours to bring his men six miles to the battlefield may also have been caused by misplaced traditionalism. He did not hurry the troops forward but had them march in step, aligned, a witness said, "as on parade."[9] Clausewitz, who knew him well, later wrote that Rüchel trusted "Prussian troops using Frederician tactics with courage and determination to overcome anything that had emerged from the unsoldierly Revolution. General Rüchel," he concluded, "might have been termed a concentrated acid of pure Prussianism."[10]

As Hohenlohe's infantry waited in serried ranks for reinforcements, firing blind volleys against troops hidden in the village and the surrounding fields, they became helpless targets. Writing before the First World War, the British military historian Major-General F. N. Maude called the event, with some hyperbole, "one of the most extraordinary and pitiful incidents in military history. This line of magnificent infantry . . . stood out in the open for two whole hours . . . exposed to the merciless skirmishing fire of the French, who . . . offered no mark at all for their return fire."[11] Eventually the front gave way. Some battalions scattered, others withdrew in good order. The French pursuit was slowed by Prussian counterattacks, but a gap opened in the line and drew in troops that until then had stood fast. Thousands fled the battlefield, most in the direction of Weimar, from which Rüchel's corps was at last approaching. Rüchel might have formed a defensive line behind which Hohenlohe's forces could have reorganized, but he remained in character and attacked. His men's deliberate advance was smashed by concentric fire, Rüchel was wounded, and his corps merged with the crowds streaming away from the battlefield. Remnants reached Weimar, where Murat's lead squadrons, which occupied the town by early evening, scattered them.

The number of casualties on both sides can only be estimated. A few units reported precise figures. One French division of 11,000 men listed 2,645 killed and wounded—24 percent. Other French units had losses ranging from 7 to 19.5 percent. A Prussian regiment lost over a third of its 66 officers and ensigns.[12] Civilian deaths were few, but against the emperor's orders Weimar was looted, as Jena had been. Goethe and his household did not suffer, Hegel was told, which was not altogether true: two soldiers forced their way into Goethe's house, drank wine, rushed into his bedroom, and threatened him with bayonets or short sabers before being persuaded to leave—events Goethe summarized in his diary: "5:30 Chasseurs arrive. 7:00 o'clock fire [breaks out in the street], looting, terrible night. Our house preserved through courage and good luck." "No one," Hegel noted, "imagined war as we have seen it."[13]

During the fighting at Jena, another battle took place eleven miles to the north at Auerstedt. The day before, Davout's corps had turned southwest to advance against the left and rear of the forces facing Napoleon. Instead, his light cavalry unexpectedly met forward units of the main Prussian army, marching northeast, away from Jena. Intense fighting began, with both sides committing troops as they arrived. After the actions of the previous days, Davout still had 27,300 men and perhaps 44 guns with which to block Brunswick's approximately 50,000 men and 230 guns. The fight centered on a village astride the road northeast of Auerstedt. A French attempt to outflank the Prussian attack failed, in turn the attack was brought to a halt by aimed fire from infantry hidden in the fields, against which volleys had no effect. The duke sent his quartermaster-general, Scharnhorst, to restore the situation, which, though wounded, he was able to do. Shortly afterwards, Brunswick, acting like a regimental officer, sought to bring the center forward and was mortally wounded. With Scharnhorst gone, no senior staff officer was now present to restore the unity of command, or to assist Frederick William in taking control. The Prussian attacks became uncoordinated, yet they nearly broke the French lines. As the battle turned against the Prussians, the king ordered his nephew, Prince August, to attack the French with four battalions to give the main force time for an orderly retreat. In the course of the attack Clausewitz, then the prince's adjutant, formed some of the grenadiers into awkward skirmish lines to support the advance—a rare case of attempting to answer the French tactics in kind.[14] The French were too exhausted to disturb the withdrawal, except for cavalry that harried the Prussian left wing throughout the evening, pursuing some units seven miles or more beyond the battlefield.

The main army's effort to regain its link to Berlin against a force half its strength had failed. As at Jena casualties were heavy—for the French over 25 pecent, more than 7,000 men killed and wounded. Prussian totals were probably somewhat less than Davout's estimate of 15,000. They also lost 3,000 prisoners and 115 guns.[15] Bad as this was, worse was to follow. The king, not yet aware of Hohenlohe's defeat, directed the retreat west to Weimar instead of northeast toward Prussia. Soon the troops were overrun by fleeing remnants of Hohenlohe's command. Hours were needed to sort out the many thousands scattered over miles, and shift the retreat north. Here and there a battalion or a battery was captured by the French, but they, too, needed rest before the pursuit began in earnest with Davout heading for Berlin, which he entered unopposed on the 25th. Other forces followed the Prussian retreat in a wide northwestern curve past Magdeburg, which, like other fortresses, surrendered with little or no resistance, across the Elbe to the Baltic. Some Prussian units turned east toward Pomerania and East Prussia; 9,000 to 10,000 men under Blücher continued northwest to Lübeck. They were trailed by Bernadotte, who on November 5, after some hours of street fighting, took the town. Two days later Blücher surrendered his remaining forces. In the month since the war began, over half of the Prussian army had been destroyed, scattered, or taken prisoner, and much of the state was occupied. Only Silesia, East Prussia, and a part of the Baltic coast remained free. Yet, with Russian support, fighting continued in East Prussia through the next spring, until the tsar agreed to an armistice, and Prussia, truncated and burdened with heavy reparations, became a French satellite.

▣ 5 ▣

After the initial shock of the two disasters, the view spread among the survivors that even a better general than Hohenlohe, who should have fought nothing more than a rearguard action, would have been too weak to prevail at Jena, whereas Brunswick with his superior numbers should have succeeded at Auerstedt.[16] Two centuries later this still seems a reasonable conclusion. But what lessons could the defeat teach the defeated? What made the check at Jena worse than it might have been? And why was the main Prussian army unable to push aside its outnumbered opponent at Auerstedt? Certainly Napoleon made the difference—but not at Auerstedt, which he never saw. Hohenlohe had been a poor commander; but senior appointments could go wrong under any system. Nor was the Duke of Brunswick's fatal wound an avoidable flaw; it merely exemplified the randomness of combat. Other elements of the two battles, however, could be studied and corrected.

In 1806 the French were the better integrated and mobile force, against which the less flexible and slower Prussians, with their uncertain strategic concepts, would not necessarily lose but were at a disadvantage. When Brunswick rejected a strategy based on maneuver rather than battle and moved against the French before they were assembled, his army could not respond. That is not to say either that the French were invincible or that their greater mobility and more versatile use of terrain were now the only model to follow. British and Hanoverian troops had been effective against the republic and continued to be so against the empire, with relatively few adjustments in tactics or organization. They were particularly strong in the defensive; forming squares to repel cavalry charges remained an effective measure far into the nineteenth century. But the structure of the British army was more flexible than that of the Prussians, and in some respects the British *had* changed. Wellington's staff, to mention only this point, was no longer the staff of an earlier Brunswick at Minden; and in Spain and at Waterloo the British generally fought alongside allies, who—however irritating they might be—added tactical versatility. What mattered was to recognize that the enemy had adopted important new ways of fighting, and to respond to them in organization, training, tactics, and strategy, even if this required changes elsewhere as well.

CHAPTER I

After 1806 it was as important to eliminate the formalism that ruled the Prussian army as it was to alter the army's organization, strategic outlook, and operational and tactical doctrine. Too often the army was run like a platoon. Senior commanders and subordinates alike tended to obey orders literally. At the same time individual and institutional rigidity coexisted with the acceptance of social prerogatives in appointments, promotions, and discipline, which might further diminish efficiency.

To improve organization and tactics, privileges had to be reduced and behavior changed. Discipline and treatment of the rank and file, laws that exempted segments of the population from military service, the status of the technical services—all needed to be dealt with. A later chapter will address these issues. Here it is enough once more to note the interaction between social and military elements, which made any change in the army more difficult.

Even before 1806 some officers recognized these links, and many more came to see them afterwards. They were equally apparent to the great German liberal historians of the nineteenth century, preeminently Johann Gustav Droysen and Hans Delbrück, whose interpretations were ideologically sharpened by such Marxist writers as Friedrich Engels in the 1840s and Franz Mehring before the First World War. A very different conclusion was developed by officers of the historical sections of the Prussian and, after 1871, the German General Staff. Their usually very competent publications largely ignored or even denied the significance of the French amalgamation of close and open order.[17] The main cause of the Prussian defeat, they declared in formulations that continued to be used in official histories down to the Third Reich, was poor leadership. Flaws in organization, doctrine, and training contributed to the outcome but meant little compared to the shortcomings of the senior generals. The most prominent representative of this view was Count Schlieffen, who as chief of the General Staff and after his retirement in 1906 wrote a number of intellectually and stylistically brilliant historical studies. His analysis of Hannibal's generalship had, as we know, a bearing on his strategic plans against France in a new war. In his essays on the war of 1806, which take up some eighty pages in his collected works, he concluded firmly that "it was not the officers'... lack of bravery, nor antiquated tactics that defeated the Prussians at Jena, but Napoleon's determination and energy, his vast numerical superiority, and the endless mistakes of the senior Prussian commanders."[18]

Schlieffen and the many who agreed with him seem not to have realized that their views placed them in opposition to their predecessors who after the defeats of 1806 rebuilt the army. Schlieffen's conclusion is particularly interesting when we compare it to his analysis of the battles in earlier pages of the same essays. To take only Hohenlohe's men facing skirmishers at Jena, Schlieffen writes: "The French infantry hidden in the fields and behind hedges and walls [of the village], directed ... accurate fire at the Prussian and Saxon battalions, lined up like practice targets that couldn't be missed, [and] that by the numbers, from left to right, fired one ineffective volley after another."[19] We might almost be reading Major-General Maude.

Clearly, Hohenlohe should not have attacked. But once his lines faced infantry in open order, the prevailing doctrine, as Schlieffen notes, left the Prussian lines helpless. The disjunction between Schlieffen's recognition and his contrary conclusion that ineffective tactics were not a major factor in the defeat justifies our seeking an explanation beyond his words, and we find it in the times in which he wrote—the first years of the twentieth century, when the military leadership of the German empire was coming under criticism for allowing caste considerations limit the army's growth, by insisting, at least in Prussia, on an officer corps drawn from the upper and professional middle classes; for emphasizing ceremony over realistic training; and for exposing recruits to harsh and insulting treatment. To the assertion of the military reformers after 1806 that the army could not be modernized without changing society and state, Schlieffen a century later responded by emphasizing strategy and leadership, which took the problem out of society and politics—in much the same way, we might think, as his plan of attacking France through Belgium, which he bequeathed to the generation of 1914, ignored its likely political consequences. Schlieffen surveyed the issue from the high perch of generalship and was unwilling publicly to acknowledge the political and social implications of doctrine and drill. His intellectual rectitude suggests that this was not a conscious decision. He may not have been aware of the extent to which ingrained beliefs affected his interpretations of the present and past—which takes us back to the basic issue, the problem of recognizing and coming to terms with the new, the acting individual's difficulty, which is matched by the difficulty historians experience, who are also never free of preconceptions and, indeed, prejudice.

More versatile tactics would not have given Prussia victory at Jena and Auerstedt, but together with less mechanical discipline and the encouragement of initiative disaster could have been prevented. A willingness to examine French practice systematically might have modified if not replaced the ultimately unquestioning trust in one's own ways. Instead, with some exceptions, the army regarded the French as an imperfect copy of itself, an assumption that made it difficult to understand the enemy's conduct so that it could be adopted or countered effectively. Schlieffen's recognition of Prussian tactical shortcomings, followed by his inability to draw the consequences, also illustrates the difficulties of the cognitive process in general—whether in Wilhelmine Germany, in the Napoleonic era, or in other conditions and at other times.

The arts cast light on the past. They bring together seemingly disparate areas of thought and action and may reveal new facts. More often they confirm and enlarge on what is already known or suspected. An investigation of the challenge of innovation in 1806 will find it useful to turn to the products of literary and visual culture of those years as indicators of German reactions to the war—one of many such gauges, among them the universities, individuals and institutions engaged in manufacturing and finance, and local and regional representative assemblies. In a circumscribed study, which cannot address the full range of the evidence, the arts may here stand in for the rest. They reflect and document attitudes of their times—openly or implicitly, favorably or critically. Sometimes they also interpret and support ideas, and whether they record or support, they influence the attitudes and vocabulary of men and women trying to understand and respond to innovation. Historians of war, intent on the hard specifics of combat, often push aside such indeterminacies as the culture of those whose wars they study. They concentrate on violence in its overt forms and may ignore evidence that is relevant even if it does not fit expected categories.

How works of art and literature address war also tells us something about the works as such. They, too, are part of history—even, perhaps especially, when the artist's creative energy takes them beyond documentation. Jacques-Louis David's 1812 portrait of Napoleon, powerful in his uniform, his masculinity emphasized, yet with stockings slightly loose and wrinkled, is a remarkable psychological and historical interpretation, as well as a very good painting. That a great artist painted the picture makes it an even richer historical source. It may be objected that a portrait by someone of David's stature is particularly subjective, and its information therefore unreliable. On the contrary, our knowledge of the artist and his work makes it likely that when he paints the emperor, who leaves his reports and maps for a few minutes to pose for him, the result deserves attention as much for what David tells us about Napoleon as for the brushstrokes with which he composes his image.

The people to whom the reactions in print and paint to the campaign were addressed belonged mainly to the German middle and upper classes. They made up the reactive, educated, engaged eighteenth-century public Habermas contrasts with the passively receptive media public of the Industrial Revolution. Except for officers and their families, war was rather remote to these privileged groups. Throughout Germany, the middle range of society was largely exempt from military service—not least in Prussia, where the rank and file was made up almost entirely of unfree peasants, the urban poor, and foreign mercenaries. It was also a socially and politically fragmented public—socially, because much of the caste system of the ancien régime remained in place; politically, because even after the collapse of the Holy Roman Empire of the German Nation and Napoleon's reorganization of Central Europe, people lived under the laws of dozens of states and principalities. In 1806 neither these governments nor their subjects were unanimous in reacting to the defeat Prussia had suffered. Their responses were determined by politics, but also by cultural attitudes—and these were in flux. The war of 1806 coincided with great intellectual and cultural changes in Germany. The Enlightenment's optimistic belief in normative universal values, which reason and education would spread to advance mankind toward a more rational world, had faded. Gradually, never completely, it was replaced by a new appreciation of differences among cultures and individuals striving to achieve their full potential, whatever that might be—new ideas that emphasized the particular over the general.

Prussia, however, was the enlightened state par excellence. Her defeat came in a time that increasingly questioned her values. For more than a century her rulers had created institutions and regulations that channeled the individual's abilities and energies toward the increase of state power. Prussia exemplified a system of government that Hegel now characterized as "mechanistic, supremely rational . . . , trusting nothing that it did not order and carry out itself—dismissive of any individual initiative."[2] Her army reflected her government. German reactions to Prussia's defeat were thus complicated by questions concerning her bureaucratic and military institutions, which tamed and reeducated high as well as low. As the state supported the old elites and confirmed them in their status, it disciplined them into obedience. Prussia, it was said, was tradition marching in lockstep. But in parts of Germany the old authorities with their social and economic controls were now removed, and many Germans welcomed the change. A novel by Heinrich Heine, *Das Buch Legrand*, in which he recalls his youth in Düsseldorf, captures the exhilaration people felt as the French broke the traditional elites' hold on power and eliminated legal distinctions between social groups. "Legrand" in the book's title refers, of course, to Napoleon; but also to a drummer, Monsieur Legrand, quartered in the house of Heine's parents when the French occupied Düsseldorf in 1806. Eventually the town became the capital of a new grandduchy, a French satellite, patched together from Prussian and other German territories. Monsieur Legrand, Heine writes, knew little German, but with his drumbeats he explained the battle of Jena to the young Heine—"the Prussians had been dumb, dumb, dumb"—and his drum needed no words to make the meaning of "equality," "fraternity," and "hang aristocrats from the lamppost" very clear.[3]

Heine's memories, enveloped in a thin shell of fiction, reflect a time when Germans could admire the revolution and the emperor who brought it to them. They document a historical force of greater significance than does his more famous evocation of the Napoleonic legend, his ballad of two grenadiers returning from Russian captivity, who learn that their emperor is defeated and exiled. One of them asks to be buried in French soil: when the emperor rides over his grave, the dead grenadier will rise and again follow him.[4] In contrast to the ballad's romantic longing for the vanquished hero, Heine's novel celebrates a source of German liberalism and its early flowering, a major, if not a dominant, force in the country's history from then on.

At the beginning of the nineteenth century, the admiration many Germans felt for French reforms, and their criticism of Prussia's rigid social and economic controls, and of the absolutism and dynastic interests dominant in most German states, were linked to a broad cultural patriotism, the sense that Germany's political fragmentation did not deny an underlying unity. Hegel could mock the feebleness of German political institutions and their shortsighted policies, while regretting that the recent wars had "robbed Germany of some of her most beautiful lands [and] of several million of her inhabitants."[5] But German political liberalism, which the French Revolution had fostered, began to shift its orientation in response to the wars of 1805 and 1806, to French expansion, and to Napoleon's later campaigns, in which thousands of German conscripts died for the bloated empire the revolution had become. The early cosmopolitan idealism that animated some Germans was replaced by a narrower patriotism—it could happen that supporters of the revolution twenty years later reappeared as xenophobic agitators. Within this cultural and at times already political self-identification, the reactions to the war of 1806 in art and literature ranged from objective reportage to advocacy of reform, whether under French auspices, as in Heine's novel, or by Germans, and to increasingly belligerent demands for German autonomy.

▨ I ▨

Soon after the campaign of 1806, the Saxon artist Christian Gottfried Geissler, who had watched French troops enter

FIGURE I

Christian Gottfried Geissler, *French Infantry Entering Leipzig*, 1807

Leipzig after the Battle of Jena, made an engraving of the event, which was widely reprinted (fig. I).[6] The image is something of an ethnographic study. It informs the German public of the strange military tribe now crisscrossing the country, its members conspicuously lacking the uniformity of appearance and movement expected of the military. The soldiers, some but not all with plumes on their shakos, are walking, not aligned and marching in step as the Prussian reserves had marched in their too slow advance at Jena. They carry their muskets any which way, by the barrel or butt, the weapon easily turned into a skewer for loaves of bread or a cured ham. A man in the foreground, a chicken tied to his pack, has gathered other loot in a cloth. Another has stuck a large bottle in the back pocket of his greatcoat. On the right several men have stepped out of the ragged column to buy drinks from a young woman, who to make the pleasure complete is also embraced by one of the soldiers, while another seems to be making friends with a small boy, just as Monsieur Legrand made friends with the young Heinrich Heine.

French and German accounts of the time indicate that Geissler's depiction is realistic and evenhanded. His engraving is certainly not a call to action, not even a moral condemnation of the widespread theft it documents. For a counterpart in another medium, here is a work by a local poet on the sack of Jena and Weimar, one of several on the subject published in these days. In seventy-seven clumsy stanzas, the outrage is detailed and summarized:

> And the plundering continued,
> Three times four-and-twenty hours,
> Everything without exception
> Stole they from us, rich or poor.
> If three men went out the door,
> All at once came in six more.[7]

Frank enough, yet no one is blamed. Instead, the poem treats looting, stealing, setting fire to buildings, some incidental killing, war itself, as acts of nature, a new reality to be accepted. One verse praises French officers for putting out fires their men had set, which may explain why the French authorities, who of course took for granted that armies lived off the land, allowed this broadsheet to be published and distributed. To understand and overcome the tribulations war had visited on the town, the poem counsels not revenge or political action, but a renewed commitment to God.

A second engraving by Geissler, hand-colored by one of the many pieceworkers the publisher employed, is a dramatic scene, no doubt an invented episode in the retreat after the battles of Jena and Auerstedt (fig. 2). Blücher's corps, closely pursued by the French, has reached Lübeck. Street fighting is in progress but will soon end in yet another Prussian rout. Geissler's rendering of uniforms, no less detailed here than in the earlier print, allows us to identify the units of most of the men milling about—a primitive but effective means of claiming factual accuracy. On the right, three French infantrymen are firing; a fourth has already broken into a house and is about to drop his loot from a window. From other windows people are firing into the crowd. Farther back, a French hussar, swinging his saber, rides into the smoke covering the street. Across the street a Prussian hussar struck by a bullet is falling. Behind him a French gunner fires one of the light cannon attached to the infantry. Four men dominate the foreground—two standing and two who with their horses have fallen on the cobblestones. On the left, a bearded man on his knees bleeds from a cut on the temple. In the center a *chasseur à cheval*, his back to the viewer, faces a tall hussar, who holds a naked infant in his hands. On the

FIGURE 2

Christian Gottfried Geissler, *Scene in Lübeck*, ca. 1806–1807

right, an officer of the Polish Legion in French service offers the hussar a covering for the infant—a cloth bloodied by his wounds. The child has become separated from his parents, the man and woman on the far right, civilians caught up in the violence. For a moment the four French soldiers in the center are turning away from the fighting around them to save a new life.

CHAPTER 2

By its accidental presence in this scene of violence and death, the infant has awakened a sense of humanity in the soldiers, who interrupt their bloody work for the child's sake—and for their own. That the soldiers are foreigners fighting Germans underlines the print's message of a good transcending the physical and emotional violence of combat. In this crisis the parents, like all civilians, are helpless, but the child—and the religious allusion would have been clear—holds out hope for life beyond war. To its buyers the print must have appealed for its drama and mayhem; it would also have reminded some of the human costs of war, and perhaps suggested a different view of the reasons men fought in 1806.[8]

Another incident, this one not invented, was the death of Prince Louis Ferdinand at Saalfeld on October 10. It became a popular subject, repeatedly pictured in France and Germany. An early example is a tinted engraving after a work by the Alsatian genre and battle painter Jacques François Swebach (fig. 3), its composition based on the now classical paintings of cavalry clashes in the Thirty Years' War by such seventeenth-century artists as Philips Wouverman, a roiling mass of horses and men in a fantasy landscape—as accurate as the misspelled name of the engagement in the engraving's title—in its midst the prince, bareheaded, vainly parrying the fatal saber thrust. His death at the hand of a common hussar not only foretells the outcome of the battles that follow but symbolically encapsulates the entire sequence of wars since 1792.

Yet another symbolic image, also published in 1807, is an unsigned engraving of a probably fictitious incident in the

FIGURE 3
Jacques François Swebach, *The Death of Prince Louis*, 1807

Prussian retreat after Jena and Auerstedt (fig. 4). A Prussian regiment has reached the River Saale but is now surrounded. To save the regimental colors, two young ensigns, scions of well-known noble families, jump into the river with them and drown—an act reflecting the sense of honor of the old elites, but also their inability to cope with the new.[9] The engraving appeared on the back cover of a journal, *Neue Feuerbrände*, "New Torches." The name and the crossed torches underneath the picture indicate the journal's stated mission to "illuminate and consume in flames of truth" the attitudes and policies that had led to Prussia's decline. Its publisher, Friedrich von Cölln, native of one of the mini-

FIGURE 4
Unknown artist, *Saving the Colors*, 1807

states in central Germany, had, like many ambitious men, chosen a career in Prussia. As a midlevel official he came to know the state machinery and found much to question in its policies and methods. Now he wrote and published articles that among other criticism rejected the preference Prussia gave to the nobility—although Cölln himself had a title—condemned the treatment of the common soldier,

VIOLENCE IN WORDS AND IMAGES

and in often rude terms laid bare the incompetence and pretensions of the old elites. To later nationalist historians he exemplifies the unpatriotic opportunism and cozying up to the French that they claim followed the Prussian defeat. In fact, though astonishingly aggressive in his denunciations, Cölln refused to swear allegiance to the French. He was among that minority of soldiers and officials who before the war had seen weaknesses in the army and administration, but whose warnings had no impact.

In subject and approach the images we have seen are broadly representative of the mass of popular prints on war in these years. We might note that they depict war in segments, in details. More panoramic images of the time exist, but they are schematic, and generally uninformative. Battles, even Napoleonic battles fought by cohesive masses of men over relatively circumscribed areas, are difficult to record visually. Continuity of action is no problem to a novel or poem but can be shown only in a sequential work like the Bayeux Tapestry, or by compressing successive events into one. A medieval illumination relies on the viewer's readiness to imagine the passage of time separating its parts: the same page or scroll shows the advance of a group of armed men, combat, pursuit of the defeated force, and looting of its camp—the viewer adds the temporal sequence between these episodes. Later artists, captive to one or the other kind of realism, lose this alternative. They depict a battle either by showing the opposing forces at a given moment or, as we have seen, by isolating a crucial episode, the detail standing for the whole.[10]

We have moved from factual depictions of French soldiers occupying a German town to fantasy images of a real
event, the death of Prince Louis Ferdinand, of an inven-
tion, a child's life saved in a street battle, which conveys a
message of the primacy of human values over the concerns
of state and army, and of the probably imagined suicide of
two young soldiers on the cover of a journal that stated
the need for reform and innovation by sensationalizing the
flaws of the old system. In their quick response to military
and political upheaval, these popular images and broadsheets
and the many others like them expressed common senti-
ments and raised issues, directly and symbolically, that after
the first shock called for more considered artistic reaction
and interpretation. The typical gives way to the exceptional.
Of the writers and artists who answered this challenge in
an aesthetically and intellectually far-reaching manner, the
most significant and most enlightening for our purpose are
two dramatists and a painter. The first, Friedrich von Schiller, died in May 1805, sixteen months before the battles of
Jena and Auerstedt; but he reacted to the earlier Napoleonic campaigns, and his plays on the seventeenth-century
generalissimo Albrecht von Wallenstein laid the foundation
for every subsequent serious discussion of war in German
literature. A few years later Heinrich von Kleist, in his drama
Prinz Friedrich von Homburg, wrote what is at once a critique
and an apotheosis of the Prussia Napoleon defeated. Two

years after that, late in 1813, a painting by Caspar David Friedrich defined what by then was becoming a new military and political reality.

Schiller served as a regimental physician in the Württemberg army before deserting in 1782 to teach and write. For some years he was a lecturer in history at the University of Jena. One of his early poems, simply called "In a Battle," gives an archetypical account of war from the common soldiers' point of view, their fear and their resigned acceptance of death—at the time unusual in subject and approach. Schiller's writings on tyranny and freedom gained the attention of the French revolutionary government, which awarded him honorary French citizenship, even as the terror turned him against the revolution. In 1794 he began to write a play on Wallenstein—now addressing the conflicts of one individual without ignoring the feelings and actions of the mass—a project that grew into a trilogy and occupied him periodically over the next five years.

Wallenstein, an obscure Bohemian noble whose recruiting prowess raised him to command the main Hapsburg army in the first half of the Thirty Years' War, began to consider changing his allegiance to the Protestant princes and their Swedish allies, a change of front that might have ended years of destructive yet inconclusive fighting with a compromise peace. He was assassinated in 1632 on orders or with the implied consent of the Hapsburg emperor. Even as Schiller was at work on the plays, Goethe recognized that he was writing both historical and contemporary drama.

Wallenstein, he noted, was "the story of Dumouriez," the French revolutionary general who in 1793 defected to the Allies.[11] Equally obvious were parallels between Wallenstein and Napoleon, both minor nobles, whose energy and military brilliance—Schiller wrote that Wallenstein fought war in a new way—made them a threat to the established order. The conflict between the great powers and an intruder out of nowhere, whether Bohemia or Corsica, underlies the play's action. In a prologue Schiller openly states the contemporary connection, introducing Wallenstein to his audience with the words, "You know him—the creator of strong armies, idol of the camp and scourge of many countries, the adventurous son of fortune."[12]

Artists and poets are never original in every major aspect of their work, and despite the revolutionary nature of Schiller's plays, others in eighteenth-century German literature preceded him in turning politics and war into drama. Notably Lessing in 1763, in his serious comedy *Minna von Barnhelm,* discussed themes of obedience and honor at the time of the Seven Years' War—according to Goethe the first modern German play using significant motives of the contemporary world. But the French Revolution and the wars of a resurgent France against Prussia, the Hapsburg Empire, and their German and British allies exerted a deeper impact on German life than had the Seven Years' War.

Schiller's trilogy depicts Wallenstein's last days. The principal, almost the only character of the first play, *Wallenstein's Camp,* is the army, the embodiment of Wallenstein's power, and a major protagonist in the plays that follow. Nearly everyone on stage is a soldier, the most senior a sergeant-major—a perspective on the common man foretold in Schiller's early poem of battle. The men's names are not given; they are identified by their units: Dragoons, Sharpshooters, *Chasseurs*—men Wallenstein recruited throughout Europe and fused into a self-consciously cohesive force. The soldiers are aware of problems that have arisen between the court in Vienna and their commander and are troubled by the arrival at headquarters of an imperial emissary, who, it is rumored, seeks to detach several regiments to other commands, destroy the army's unity, and weaken its leader. A few civilians also appear: a peasant and his son, a woman sutler—an ancestor of Brecht's Mother Courage—and a capuchin friar, who shouts out a sermon in which he scolds Wallenstein for insufficient Catholic fervor and lazy generalship. Some soldiers defend the friar's right to speak, foretelling divisions of opinion and loyalty among Wallenstein's generals in the later plays; but most agree to draft a petition to keep the army united and deliver it to one of their regimental commanders and a favorite of Wallenstein, Max Piccolomini.

The play evokes Wallenstein as his soldiers see him, a stern but loyal father, their attachment to him, and the conflict now dividing him and the emperor. These are the central elements of the two plays that follow. Through their voices we also hear the soldiers' existential self-identification: serving under a great commander has liberated them—a claim explained in part by the low social origin of most, from which the army has raised them above the usual constraints of society. They are free to rob and kill; war has liberated them from the conventions and corruption of daily life. Above all, their courage frees them from humanity's common fear of death. Without explicitly defining it, Schiller reveals the paradox of the belief that a regimented and dangerous existence liberates—a contradiction that is resolved in the belief that whatever the external reality, inner freedom is true freedom.

Wallenstein's Camp ends with great effect by changing from dialogue to music. First one soldier, then everyone on stage, sings a paean on war as freedom, "Wohlauf Kameraden, aufs Pferd, aufs Pferd . . . ," a song that soon entered the political domain as a patriotic counterpart to Schiller's *Ode to Joy*, to universal brotherhood, which liberals were adopting as a statement of faith. When Prussia mobilized in 1806, officers and men representing the regiments of the Berlin garrison were commanded to a performance of the play, at the end of which they joined the cast in the song—high and popular culture coming together at a critical time. Here is the opening stanza in my prose translation: "Saddle up, comrades, to horse, to horse, / On to war and to freedom. / In war a man still counts, / His heart is still weighed and valued. / No-one can take his place, / He is on his own." The second verse expands on this message: "Freedom has passed from this world of lords and slaves. / . . . Only the man who can look death in the face, The soldier, is free!" And the last verse ends with the refrain: "And if you don't stake life, / You will never have gained life."

Soon after the trilogy appeared, Samuel Taylor Coleridge translated the second and third plays into English; but not the first, which he mistook for a mere introduction. On the contrary, in *Wallenstein's Camp* we come to know the characteristics and beliefs of one of the drama's major actors, the army. Rejecting the German—but not the French—reality of his time, Schiller inserts the common people in the high politics and ethics of their betters. In the succeeding two plays the army disappears from view to become the power behind the scene, a shift marked by the staging. *Wallenstein's Camp* takes place on open ground between tents. The other two plays are set in castle halls, studies, and chambers, a contrast between freedom and enclosure, which underlines Wallenstein's inability, and that of his friends and his secret enemies, to break the cycle of conspiracy and counter-conspiracy, which began with the emperor's fear that his general was gaining too much power, and Wallenstein's fear that despite his victories he would be replaced. His indifference to religious matters and to the emperor's dynastic motives deepens the division. The second play, *The Piccolominis*, is named after a general, secretly the emperor's ally, and his son, a young idealist, who cannot agree with his father and in the end seeks death in battle as an escape from the lies that surround him—echoing the song with which *Wallenstein's Camp* reaches its emotional climax. The play traces the divided loyalty of Wallenstein's officers and his failure to act decisively as control of the army slips out of his hands. In the third, concluding play, *Wallenstein's Death,* the soldiers refuse to turn against the emperor. The army's inaction is decisive. It only remains to murder Wallenstein, who to the end cannot believe he has failed. The last scenes underline his human qualities, even as his indecision reduces him from potential historical significance to failure.[13]

Wallenstein's Camp is written in informal German; even what Coleridge calls its "lilting rhymes" cannot hide a strong conversational and social realism. The other two plays are composed, again according to Coleridge, "in very polish'd Blank Verse," to which I would add the attribute of great suppleness. Complex feelings and ideas, whether of Wallenstein, his friends seeking a way through intractable situations, or the emperor's supporters who feign loyalty to their general while planning to kill him, are stated with a noble clarity. Their ideas and reflections are encased in discussions that range across broad reaches of politics and war. Schiller takes the world of his characters seriously. A reminder by Count Piccolomini to his son that "Even in war, what ultimately matters is not war" could have been written by Clausewitz. Some verses later the young Piccolomini advises that in war one should remain in communication with the enemy, so that one's policy and ultimate intentions are clear to him: "For if war does not already cease in war, from where should peace return?"[14] We may agree or not; the words express ideas about the purpose and conduct of war that are anything but simplistic. Schiller does not allot his characters a few suitable phrases as a kind of verbal costume, he gives them serious ideas to express, which are entwined with the personalities and motives of the leading and minor figures. The realities of war become part of the plays. And the plays, it is not too much to say, become part of historical reality— of the way some Germans come to think about war and the relationship between political and military power.

To illustrate this cultural penetration, here are some instances from the life of Carl von Clausewitz. Early in 1812, reacting to Napoleon's demand that Prussia supply troops to the invasion of Russia, the young Clausewitz resigned his commission in the Prussian service and left for Russia to fight against his former comrades. He explained his decision in three essays, which combine idealism with strategic and operational analyses that treat war not merely as a clash of numerically defined opponents, but also as shaped by psychological factors. In the margin of his manuscript, next to a sentence on the need to understand the character of supreme commanders, Clausewitz adds the words: "Wallenstein. Schiller."[15] Ten months later, in December, the Prussian auxiliary corps under General Yorck retreated with the *Grande Armée* from Russia. On the 29th the Prussians reached Tauroggen near the East Prussian border, as small Russian units moved between them and the French. Russian emissaries, Clausewitz now serving with them, proposed a convention to neutralize the 14,000 Prussians, which would prevent Napoleon from forming a defensive line in western Poland. Later Clausewitz recalled Yorck questioning his regimental commanders about how their men would react to abandoning the French: "More or less like Wallenstein,"

CHAPTER 2

he wrote, "General Yorck strode up and down and asked, 'What say your regiments?'"[16] After Napoleon's final defeat Clausewitz, now back in the Prussian army, served as chief of staff to his friend Gneisenau, a leader of Prussia's military reforms and commanding general in the Rhineland, acquired by Prussia at the Congress of Vienna. As conservatives in Prussia reverted to their old politics now that the French were defeated, some came to suspect Gneisenau and his staff, most of whom had been active in the reforms, of supporting liberal ideas in the new province, even of undermining the authority of the crown. They expressed their suspicions by referring to Gneisenau's headquarters as Wallenstein's camp on the Rhine. As we shall see in a subsequent chapter, Clausewitz not only takes over some of Schiller's expressions to formulate his ideas, in developing a structural analysis of war he borrows concepts from the art, literature, and aesthetic systems of his time.[17]

To the German middle classes of the later nineteenth century, Schiller became the national poet, whose life and work exemplified those special qualities that, it began to be said, distinguished Germans above others, a cultural fantasy that was to add an arrogant, dangerous note to the later drive toward unification. But neither the plays nor Schiller's other works nor his letters support this enthusiastic reading.[18] On the contrary, the trilogy is profoundly nonideological. It does not preach German nationalism—whether as a motivating force in the seventeenth century, which would have been historically absurd, or as a guide to future generations.

Here the plays concur with other works we have seen. Xenophobic voices did begin to be heard at this time, but they pointed to the future. The ideological fervor that animated the soldiers of the French Revolution, and survived as a weaker, more diffused presence in Napoleon's armies, was in Germany never countered by an equivalent ideological élan. Since contingents from several German states fought under Napoleon until the fall of 1813, German xenophobia in those years could hardly have been more than a noisy, marginal force.

※ 3 ※

In contrast to the quick triumph of Schiller's trilogy, Kleist's play *Prinz Friedrich von Homburg,* hampered by censorship, achieved recognition slowly. Unlike Schiller, who came to the topic of high politics and civil–military relations from the outside, Kleist wrote about his own world. He descended from a Pomeranian family, first documented in the thirteenth century, that provided hundreds of officers, some of the highest rank, to the Brandenburg and Prussian armies. Kleist served against the French Revolution as an officer in the 1st Footguards before resigning his commission to study and write. Background, experience, and connections in the army and at court gave him insight into politics and the continuing debates over changes in army organization and operational and tactical doctrine, and his plays and novels, although usually placed in the past, are suffused with contemporary issues and references. In an earlier play, *The*

Battle of Arminius—completed at the end of 1808 under the impact of the Spanish insurrection and Austria's and Russia's impending war against Napoleon—Kleist addresses German political disunity in the face of French aggression by going back to the Augustan age, and Roman expansion into Central Europe. Arminius temporarily unites the German tribes, lures the Roman legions of Quintilius Varus deep into the German forest, and destroys them. The play reflects and is meant to inspire the present. Together with some patriotic poems Kleist wrote in the following months, it gives full scope to his thinking and writing in emotional extremes, his creative compulsion to cross all borders in his language, which reappears in more disciplined form in *The Prince von Homburg,* written between 1809 and 1811.

Set in seventeenth-century Brandenburg, the true scene of the play is the Prussian monarchy that emerged from it. The plot is an invented episode in the war of 1675 between the Swedes, since the Thirty Years' War established in northern Germany, and the elector of Brandenburg—one of the seven German princes who elect the emperor of the Holy Roman Empire of the German Nation—who is forcing them back toward the Baltic. It opens at night in the garden of a chateau Brandenburg troops occupied some hours earlier. The elector, his wife, his niece Natalie, and members of the court come upon the Prince von Homburg, commander of the cavalry, who, weary from the day's fighting, rests under an oak tree—stage directions specify "half awake, half asleep." Caught in dreams of glory, he twists a laurel branch into a wreath. To test the depth of his trance, the elector takes the wreath and hands it to Natalie, who holds out the wreath to the prince. Homburg takes it, and with it one of her gloves. When he wakes up, wreath and glove in his hand, he cannot separate dream from reality. He joins other officers to hear the dispositions for the coming battle, an envelopment to trap the enemy against a river. Full success depends on the prince's not attacking until given the order. But in his continued dreamlike state he attacks too early. The Swedish army is defeated yet escapes across the river. Homburg is court-martialed and condemned to death.

So far we have witnessed a conflict over the meaning of literal obedience. Or so it seems. Captivated by his dream, the prince ignores the dispositions for the battle and attacks prematurely. But Kleist adds another reason for the prince's action, which does not stand out in the hurried reports of events given to the elector's wife and members of the court by a witness, a statement the significance of which readers generally ignore.[19] At the start of the fighting, the elector's equerry persuades his master to exchange his white horse for the equerry's chestnut. Soon afterwards the equerry is killed, and witnesses who see the man on the white horse fall believe him to be the elector. It is further reported that in his anger and despair over the elector's death, the prince attacks and drives the Swedes back. In short, the prince disobeys orders out of love for the man who then condemns him to death. The conflict over command and discipline turns into a drama of emotions. The dense interaction of feelings that runs through the play thickens further, but the addition is never overtly mentioned in the arguments over the prince's sentence of death. It is a marginal reference characteristic of Kleist's anything but simple approach to human relationships, and it points again to the contact between Clausewitz and the new emphasis in the arts and scholarship on character, temperament, and feeling. Clausewitz does not cite Kleist as he cites Schiller; but he regards it not only as natural but as essential to bring emotional factors far beyond such matters as the soldiers' discipline and morale into the structural analysis of war. As we shall see with greater specificity in the fourth chapter of this study, aesthetics strongly marked Clausewitz's ideas—to the point of influencing both content and forms of his theories.[20]

The prince, shocked by the sentence of death, at first assumes it is merely a symbolic act. Then he learns that the elector has signed the sentence. On his way to the elector's wife to seek her help, he passes the grave being dug for him and panics—for many, perhaps especially when the play was first performed, its dramatic and troubling high point. "Since I saw my grave," the prince tells the electress, "I want only to live, and won't ask whether honorably or not."[21] Neither she nor her husband can believe that he would beg for his life. Natalie, who loves him, is amazed that he "now thinks of nothing but to save himself." The psychic disintegration of an important soldier is answered by the extreme rigidity of his sovereign. To justify condemning a victorious general, the elector argues that the state would collapse without law, to which Natalie presciently replies: "The state you are founding [that is, Prussia] will survive far worse than this unasked-for victory." The elector's officers also intercede, and do so bluntly. An old cavalry colonel tells him that not his will but the country's good should be the highest law. What matters is to defeat the enemy, regardless of rules: does he want to turn the army into a lifeless tool, he asks the elector, "like the sword dangling from your golden belt?" At last the elector decides that if the prince believes his sentence to be unjust, he will pardon him. But Homburg has recovered self-control and now accepts the sentence: "to triumph over one's own weakness means more than gaining a cheap triumph in battle." He follows the young Piccolomini in *Wallenstein's Death* and chooses inner freedom.

Unlike Schiller's officers, who talk in phrases of ample nobility, Kleist's men and women speak in plainer terms, which reveal their psychology with shattering immediacy. Conversations erupt in a cross fire of short phrases, even of single words, interspersed with longer expositions of ideas and feelings, whose poetic charge comes from metaphors that rise from common images. When after the clash of opinions in army and at court the prince is led blindfolded to the place of execution, he pauses for a brief monologue: his recognition that he deserves to be punished for his disobedience even as he wins the battle will, he declares, bring him lasting fame.

Now, immortality, you are all mine!
Your light, as of a thousand suns,

streams into my blindfolded eyes.

My shoulders become wings,

On which my spirit soars

through boundless realms of silence.

As from a ship, abducted by the wind,

We see the busy harbor slip from sight,

So does my life fade in the gathering dusk.

Colors I still perceive, and shapes,

And now fog covers all.[22]

The elector, however, having experienced his own learning process, decides to pardon the prince. Immortality comes to Homburg for asking to die and living nevertheless. The blindfold is taken from his eyes, he realizes he has been pardoned, faints, and as cannon fire announcing the next battle brings him back to consciousness, he asks, as at the opening of the play: "Is it a dream?" "What else?" answers an officer, while others shout "to battle, to victory . . . ; into the dust the enemies of Brandenburg!"

The references to the present and recent past were plain to everyone who read the play or saw it performed.[23] Homburg might have been inspired by Prince Louis Ferdinand, whose death at Saalfeld in 1806, some claimed, was caused by his acting against orders. He also evokes Frederick the Great, who as a young man was court-martialed for trying to escape his tyrannical father. The rejection of literal and mechanical obedience pointed to the Prussian army of 1806, and it is not surprising that the work's critical treatment of politically sensitive matter blocked its immediate success. It was soon performed in Berlin on the private stage of Prince Radziwill, husband of Prince Louis Ferdinand's sister, and some members of the court, among them Clausewitz's wife, a close friend of the Prussian princess to whom Kleist dedicated the play, may have read a manuscript copy; but not until 1821, years after Kleist's death, was it printed and publicly staged, after which it gradually entered the classical canon of German drama. The difficulties in its path say nothing about the play, much about its audience. In 1822 it could still be banned in Vienna, Archduke Charles declaring that it was improper for a theater to show an officer begging for his life. For a performance in Berlin in 1828, the offending scenes were partly rewritten, which did not keep the king from instructing the director of the Royal Theater (incidentally, Clausewitz's brother-in-law) never again to present it. Almost a century later, William II could praise the play as one of his favorites, except, he said, for the infamous scene of the prince's cowardice, which might easily be cut.

The kaiser responded to the staged military world of his ancestor, the great elector. The play, however, is more than historical drama capped with a patriotic appeal or alternately psychological combat between a younger and an older man. Kleist criticizes the formalism of the Prussian army in which he himself had served, and he asks questions basic to the conduct of war: How restrictive is an order? How wide the scope of individual initiative? But, Kleist also tells us, in their meaning and dynamic these issues are of greater than military relevance; they define personality and belong to human interaction. As Friedrich Gundolf noted in the 1920s, in the guise of a clash between a Prussian soldier-king and a poetic hero of German classicism, the play addresses the eternal conflict between law and passion.[24] By treating war as the surface layer of deeper, universal forces, or as a stage on which these forces meet, Kleist breaks down the social isolation of war—the separation Frederick the Great defined with the statement that it was his dearest wish to fight his wars without the burgher in town and the peasant on his acre being aware of it—and turns war into a part of everyone's existence. In *The Prince von Homburg,* war, in its glory and its psychic and physical awfulness, comes to stand for life itself.

■ 4 ■

A similar expansion of meaning, again linked to, even determined by, conditions at the time of its creation, occurs in Caspar David Friedrich's painting *The Chasseur in the Forest.* After preliminary studies in the summer of 1813, he completed the work early the following year—its creation coincides with the fall campaign of 1813, culminating in the Allied advance into France, but precedes the last decisive battles and the occupation of Paris in April 1814.

Friedrich became widely known in 1809 with his landscape *The Cross in the Mountains,* a painting that assumes the form and, some thought, the function of a religious shrine. His art accords with the decline of normative late-Enlightenment values and the rise of a new faith in the

particular and subjective that I mentioned earlier.[25] He turns
a bush or tree, rock or stretch of beach into pantheistic sym-
bols, which could also take on a political cast—a process
Goethe, though valuing the artist, somewhat dismissively
hyphenated as "new-German-religious-patriotic art." In his
work, Friedrich seeks to close the separation between art
and viewer. Figures, their back toward us, looking at what is
beyond them in the painting, may be more than reference
points: they represent the viewer. A path running from the
bottom frame of a landscape to its center has us imagine
ourselves walking through the painting, its rutted path leading who knows where. Friedrich and Kleist could not have
been less alike as artists and individuals, yet they were linked
by interests and sensibilities: possibly inspired by Kleist's play
on Arminius, Friedrich painted two landscapes of the hero's
tomb, which echo Kleist's celebration of his triumph over
the Romans deep in the German forest. Kleist wrote approv-
ingly of Friedrich's emotionally powerful new art; and several
of the painter's metaphoric seascapes of ships leaving harbor
and disappearing in the mist turn the Prince von Homburg's
paean on life departing into visible reality:

> As from a ship abducted by the wind,
> We see the busy harbor slip from sight,
> So does my life fade in the gathering dusk.

In its contemporary specificity, conveyed in universal terms,
The Chasseur in the Forest is a painted counterpart of Kleist's
plays. It differs by not wearing the mask of history, of past

epochs, nor does it match the violent rhetoric of *The Battle of Arminius,* or—to look beyond Kleist—the effusions of a new liberation poetry that erupted after Prussia joined Russia in the war against Napoleon, whose practitioners interpret war as a natural cataclysm, with such lines as "Rage storm, rage! The people rise!" *The Chasseur in the Forest* sounds a very different note (fig. 5).

On a narrow opening in a dense stand of firs, their branches and the ground lightly covered with snow, a man walks into the forest. We see him from the back. His crested helmet marks him as a French *chasseur à cheval,* an identity his cavalry saber and boots confirm. His horse is not in sight; it is dead or has run off, and gone with it is much of the chasseur's fighting strength. Behind him are three tree stumps, a raven perched on one of them. Even without this symbol of misfortune in the midst of other marks of death—the tree stumps and broken branches, but also of the promise of new life held out by three young firs growing between them—we know that we are in the presence of tragedy. The man alone on alien, immeasurable ground, which may hide unseen dangers, will meet death—in the German expression, which the painting re-creates, "geht seinem Tod entgegen"—and goes toward his death in the German forest, as Quintilius Varus did 1800 years earlier. That his short cloak is also green not only is historically accurate but underlines his union with the forest, with fate. Contemporary opinion was in no doubt about the work's meaning. A review of the Berlin exhibition in which the painting was shown in 1814 explains, "A French

FIGURE 5

Caspar David Friedrich, *The Chasseur in the Forest*, 1813–1814

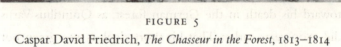

chasseur walking alone through the snowy fir forest hears his dirge sung by a raven."[26] To which we, after two centuries, might add how remarkable it is that in this very still painting, with the barely perceptible motion of the sole figure in it, the artist conveys the killing and maiming of hundreds of thousand French, German, and Russian soldiers.

At the time Friedrich painted *The Chasseur*, the painting was more a prediction of the future than a celebration of victory already won, and regardless of the bombastic interpretations the Wilhelmine Empire and later the Third Reich bestowed on the work, glorying in its deep "Germanic" feeling for nature linked to the doom of the hated national enemy, there is nothing triumphant about it: we see a human being in crisis, alone. As Wallenstein's soldiers sing, in war man "is on his own." That the painting depicts both its overt theme, the war against Napoleon, and the human condition is an attribute of its depth and power, just as *The Prince von Homburg* continues to be acted and read today because in it Kleist lays bare universal feelings beneath the political-military conflicts shaking some small state in northern Germany.

▨ 5 ▨

The adhesion of war to normal existence, which the painting exemplifies, its use of war as a metaphor of the human condition, is historically significant, a significance that the works we have discussed help us to recognize and understand. To Friedrich, as to Schiller and Kleist, war is not the only or even the preferred metaphor for life. But his painting and their plays help to break down the social and emotional isolation of war that for the middle classes had been part social fact, part cultural hope in the years before the French Revolution, an amalgamation that together with much else signals the recognition by society of a new reality created by the revolution: war is not only a matter for a military elite and the peasants, serfs, and poor of the rank and file. Nationalism and conscription bring war to everyone. The images we have seen, the plays, and Friedrich's painting reflect and reinforce this expansion.

Artists and writers had, of course, addressed war before the 1790s, but for different reasons, and with a different understanding of the subject. Hundreds of genre scenes of war were painted and engraved in the seventeenth and eighteenth centuries—dramatic episodes of combat or panoramas of battle—which hung in the salons of the well-to-do as reminders of the dangerous world outside: costumed *frissons* or *memento moris*. Rarely did these images say anything about war itself. In literature, too, war tended to be treated as a challenge to the hero's idealism or sense of adventure rather than in its own right. Then gradually war ceased to be a colorful backdrop or moral stimulus and, as in some previous eras, again became a protagonist—notably in Voltaire's *Candide,* or in a play mentioned earlier, Lessing's *Minna von Barnhelm,* in which the conflict between obedience and honor rises to sublime comedy. In Germany Lessing's work inspired feeble copies. A new literary genre appeared on the stage, the so-called soldiers' play, a stumbling forerunner of the intellectual and poetic concentration on war in the works of Schiller, Kleist, and Friedrich. The treatment of war as a part of the human experience reaches a new level in Germany at a time in which ideologically, politically, and socially war expands its reach and takes on new forms.

Kleist's *Battle of Arminius* glories in the human slaughter in war, a subject he comes to treat stoically in *The Prince von Homburg*. This particular motif is absent in the popular images we have seen, which range from uncritical reportage to criticism of the old order—in the engraving of the two ensigns drowning themselves to save the colors—and even to a kind of moral commentary on the cost of war in Geissler's invented scene of an infant saved in the streets of Lübeck. But an emphasis on bloodshed is rare in this genre, at least until reports and drawings of the Russian campaign reach Central and Western Europe.

Nor is the human cost of war emphasized in more demanding art—no artist etched a German counterpart of Goya's *Disasters of War*. German paintings and prints show corpses as mere supernumeraries in the panorama of battles or in the glorification of a commander. Much the same is true in France. Rare are works like the paintings entered in an official competition on "Napoleon on the Battlefield of Eylau," held in Paris soon after the costly battle in East Prussia in February 1807. The prize-winning paintings, by Gros and Meynier among others, show Napoleon after the battle, raising his arm "over the world" as Hegel saw him on the eve of Jena, but now bringing "help and consolation," according to the terms of the contest, "to the innumerable victims of combat." The emperor dominates, yet the paintings are covered with wounded and dying men, and corpses already robbed of their clothes. The intention is to glorify Napoleon, here in a beneficent mood; but however nobly he is depicted, the nude bodies could also raise questions about the slaughter and the man who caused it. This touches on the relationship of ruler and ruled. In Germany after 1806 the issue had not reached a degree of intensity comparable to that in France in 1789, but in the end it could not be avoided in Prussia either. In various ways the reciprocal responsibilities of sovereign, subject, and society came to dominate the efforts to understand the new forms of war and find appropriate responses to them—principally in the matter of who and under what conditions owed the state the obligation of military service—a subject that will occupy us in the next chapter.[27]

Who is to serve the state as a soldier is a highly political matter. Kleist alludes to it occasionally, but it is rare for the issue to be openly addressed in the art and literature of these years. The artists whose works we have considered emphasize above all the individual; but even in this mode they send intellectual and emotional messages to the men who will respond to the challenge of Napoleonic war when they rebuild the Prussian army, and who know they must go beyond the purely military. *Wallenstein's Camp* shows them soldiers who think for themselves in place of the automata of the Prussian line laid low by skirmishers at Jena. Individualism and discipline clash and bond as equals in *The Prince von Homburg*. In *The Chasseur in the Forest*, Caspar David Friedrich takes an ancient symbol—the German forest—and turns it into a new ideal, the nation, which gives the bourgeois, until now exempt from the military, compelling ideological reasons and official compulsion to serve. These and many similar messages put into aesthetic form ideas, some of which are already held, others that are still developing. They help us understand the time in which they originate, and the people who act and react in this time. But it is left to the politician and the soldier to expand the orientation of these works. As they respond to the issues before them and to the conditions and pressures of their situation, they must translate the message sent by words and images into institutions and policies—the politician by reducing social inequality and giving the individual, of whatever class, a new reason to bear arms in the service of the state; the soldier by exploiting the potential of the new, freer individual in doctrines and methods that increase the army's effectiveness.

3

---⊠---

Responses and Reform

After the lost war, the men in tenuous charge of whatever remained of the Prussian monarchy faced a choice: accept that
the state was now a French dependency, or work to regain
its autonomy, which almost certainly meant a new war with
France. Choosing the latter course would require a thor-
ough investigation of the causes for the army's defeat, and
the development of effective countermeasures. Would relatively minor improvements in the organization and methods
of the armed forces be adequate for a new confrontation, or
was more encompassing change needed? A state in the center of the continent might answer that question differently
than would the United Kingdom or the Russian Empire.
Within the military and civil elites, resignation and acceptance of the defeat were common; but equally widespread
was the refusal to accept its consequences. In now outlining
the Prussian response, I want to go beyond the bare results to
indicate how they were developed, and some of the conflicts
and compromises that accompanied their adoption.

⊠ I ⊠

The defeat was caused not only by the superiority of the French army, rooted in the French Revolution and its consequences, but also by the Prussian government's inefficiencies in mobilizing and employing its resources. The process of regeneration therefore challenged not only technical military practices but broad social and political interests. We gain an impression of the magnitude of the issues from statements by Clausewitz, in whose life and thought the campaign of 1806 proved a defining episode. In the years that followed he wrote repeatedly about the course of the war, each time emphasizing somewhat different aspects. To mention only three of his most significant discussions: A few weeks after the defeats of Jena and Auerstedt, which had found him in the forward lines of the fighting, he sent a report on the battles to a military journal—under the circumstances a remarkably detached study of the army's operational and tactical shortcomings.[1] Twenty years later he wrote a lengthy analytical account of Prussian institutions, society, and attitudes from the end of the eighteenth century to the war of 1806 and its conduct, a merciless, often sarcastic analysis, critical of the king and others, in which he set down his considered interpretation of the disaster and its causes. The title, *Observations on Prussia in Her Great Catastrophe*, suggests his personal engagement and the breadth of his approach—part political and operational history, part history of society and mentalities, and throughout a critical analysis of a military culture

RESPONSES AND REFORM

73

the leaders of which, from the king on, had turned tradition into a routine that denied the changing times.[2] To publish this devastating judgment would have caused great offense, and in the 1830s the editors of Clausewitz's posthumous collected works still could not bring themselves to include it. The Historical Section of the General Staff finally published the book fifty-six years after Clausewitz's death, with a defensive introduction and exculpatory notes that praised the author's idealism and commitment, while attempting to disprove his accusations.

Between these extremes of a sober report on military flaws and a deeply felt cultural and institutional analysis, Clausewitz in 1813 introduced an account of the spring campaign of 1813 with an outline of the events of 1806 and the beginning of the reforms, which linked the operations of the new Prussian army in the just concluded campaign with the years of reform. His summary is a rather conventional political and military analysis, except for its identification of the psychological impact of the defeats as a major obstacle to reform. Even in this work, which was published weeks after he had written it, with its impact on public opinion in mind, sarcastic grace notes are not absent. "In the unfortunate days of Jena and Auerstedt," Clausewitz begins,

> the Prussian army lost its glory; in the retreat it fell apart. Its fortresses were given up, the state was conquered, and after four weeks of fighting little was left of either state or army.... the [armistice] completed

the misery. . . . Within a year, Prussia's glittering military state, a joy to all lovers of soldiers and war, had disappeared. Admiration was replaced by reproach and censure, homage often by humiliation. An oppressive sadness weighed on the army's morale. Finding confidence in the past was not possible; nor was hope for the future. Even that ultimate source for regaining courage, trust in particular leaders, was absent, because in the brief war no one had achieved prominence, and the few who had distinguished themselves were divided among factions holding different opinions.[3]

Clausewitz continues by noting the difficulty of correcting the many things that had been wrong and gone wrong: "In view of the army's depressed spirit, the state's weakened economy, its financial ruin, imperious interference from without and discouragement within, which blunted every energetic measure, it was hard to reach the goal we set ourselves." That goal he defined as, "Renew and encourage the army, lift its spirits, eradicate old flaws, and as it was trained and built up to the strength allowed [by France], lay the basis for a new, larger force that would be ready to spring into action at some future decisive moment." In this summary he treats the crisis of state and army largely as an institutional and political issue. He merely hints at what in his later *Observations* he explores at length: social and cultural conditions and attitudes as much as inadequate military and civil institutions and inept diplomacy caused the defeat.

And yet, even as the old system neared its end, new forces were changing society and culture, and in the *Observations* Clausewitz confronts old beliefs with new ideas that were then entering the public sphere. In works of art and literature we have seen German society trying to understand its encounter with war, the reactions of the creative imagination coinciding with a return of war to the life and culture of the middle ranges of society from which it has been largely absent since the early seventeenth century, when the Thirty Years' War had laid waste to Central Europe. New ideas and attitudes, not yet fully formed twenty years earlier, now confront the old and help shape reform.

Early, tentative steps in this effort were taken even before the armistice with France was concluded in the summer of 1807, and negotiations began that led to the Convention of Paris, under which Prussia lost half its territory to Saxony and the new creations, the Kingdom of Westphalia and the Grand-Duchy of Warsaw. For Napoleon, extending French power to the east with a truncated Prussia at the Polish border seemed for the time being more useful than the state's complete disappearance. Some senior Prussian officials and soldiers now believed that only true subservience to French policy could assure the state's continuation. Others from the first looked for ways of regaining strength and freedom of action. When Napoleon neither eliminated the Prussian monarchy altogether nor replaced its bureaucratic and military elites, this became a realistic alternative. Despite military occupation, economic exploitation, and close policing, the drive to regain independence survived and was given scope to grow.

Once on this path, how did Prussia meet the cognitive challenge of defeat? Whatever might be done would occur in a context of limited alternatives. What remained of the state was occupied by French troops from 1807 to early 1813, a heavy indemnity was imposed, the army's strength was limited to 42,000 men for the next ten years, and such auxiliary forces as a national guard were forbidden. These outside constraints were accompanied by the domestic inhibition of the pronounced traditionalist beliefs that were held by many officials and officers, as well as the monarch. Under French oversight, Frederick William III continued to head the government. He was a man of few gifts, stubborn, firmly conservative, fixated on details, suspicious even of his supporters, and notably ill at ease with activism in army and administration, which alone could restore him to power. But he would not accept defeat as final. His unwillingness to be one more figurehead in Napoleon's collection of German princelings turned out to be his main contribution to the reforms. In the awful reality of his current existence, he could be influenced, even against his convictions.

Whatever potential for action remained lay with the state's military and bureaucratic elites. Whether conservative or liberal, they had matured under the impact of Enlightenment and late-Enlightenment thought, which was given added ferment by the French Revolution and its imperial aftermath and drew additional ideas and a new dynamic from Classicism and early Romanticism. The memoranda, letters, and publications of those of its members open to new solutions are marked by humanistic ideals that oddly combine with the aim of increasing the power of the state. An example is the newspaper article "Freedom for Backs!" by Gneisenau, one of the younger leaders of military reform, in which he argues that both efficiency and decency demand the liberation of soldiers' backs from beatings by the drill sergeant.[4] He and some others drew a distinction between reforming the Prussian military and finding an effective response to new ways of fighting. One should lead to the other; nevertheless some practices were to be replaced not or not only because they were ineffective, but because they offended against human dignity—a point of view that was now assuming political significance.

To these major and shifting elements of the intellectual and cultural context must be added events before 1806. Prussia's defeat, as we know, was not a bolt out of the blue. Since 1792 France had been intermittently at war, and Prussian officers by the hundreds had served against the revolutionary armies—although, as Clausewitz noted, until 1806 their encounter with French troops was limited to the early campaigns when innovation was not as marked as it later became. Nevertheless, the experiences gained, extensively recorded in official reports, together with an always increasing stream of books, pamphlets, and articles by officers in the various armies fighting the French, laid a basis for serious, sustained analysis of the new challenges. Some innovation in the army's structure and training also occurred. No institution as large and complex as the Prussian army could have remained unchanged in these eventful years, even if the changes introduced before 1806 neither were fundamental nor revealed a unified vision.

⬛ 2 ⬛

Within these large, often impersonal forces, a chance event did much to determine the direction and character of the eventual response. The campaigns against the French in the 1790s, together with the literature on these campaigns, brought a man to the Prussian service, and there to a position of influence, from which he was able to guide the army's regeneration. How Gerhard Scharnhorst attracted the attention of Berlin takes us deep into the social reality of the German military world at the time. His father, a free peasant, had risen to sergeant in the Hanoverian army and, on inheriting some landed property, was lifted—barely—into the middle range of society.[5] The son attended a military academy, was commissioned, taught in a regimental school, and began to write on military affairs. His abilities were recognized, but in the most caste-ridden officer corps in Germany his prospects for advancement were poor. Then the revolutionary wars began. Scharnhorst distinguished himself in action and as advisor to senior commanders. After the Peace of Basle in 1795, he became known beyond the borders of Hanover as an author on contemporary war and a publisher of military journals. In 1797 he was offered a Prussian commission, in

accord with the long-standing Prussian practice of recruiting able foreigners. Promotion to lieutenant colonel checked
this attempt, but it was renewed in 1800, and Scharnhorst
accepted the offer once his demands were met: a pension on
retirement, transferable to his wife and children, and elevation to the nobility since, he wrote, without a title his sons
could not expect a good career in the Prussian army.[6]

In Berlin Scharnhorst was made head of a military school,
later called the Academy for Young Infantry and Cavalry
Officers, founded to raise the professional competence of
junior officers and prepare some for service on the General Quartermaster Staff. This was another step on the way
from ad hoc arrangements toward the permanent body that
grew into the general staff as the planning—and eventually the command—center of the army. Among successful
candidates in 1801 was the twenty-one-year-old Lieutenant
Clausewitz. Scharnhorst also served as director of the semi-
official Military Society, a group of officers and officials of
all ranks he helped found to discuss military affairs and past
campaigns.[7] With his contempt of dogma, his testing of sup-
posedly scientific principles of war against practical reality,
and his habit of analyzing military policy and operations
within their historical and social context, he soon put his
mark on the academy and the Military Society. Representative of his outlook is the essay he published in 1798 while
still in Hanover, on "The General Reasons for the Successes
of the French in the Revolutionary War," a study soon well
known, and a classic of comprehensive military-political

analysis. In it he interprets the French army's changes in organization, operations, and tactics in conjunction with conscription and new promotion policies, which, he notes, were in turn the products of social change and a changed relationship of the subject—now citizen—and the state.[8]

Shortly before the war of 1806, Scharnhorst submitted a memorandum to two of the army's leading figures, the Duke of Brunswick and the king's first adjutant, which raised the question then central to Prussia's existence: how to fight a defensive war against the far stronger French empire. Not only by enlarging the standing army, he answered, but by creating a "National Militia." The increase in numerical strength mattered, but more important seemed to him the impact a citizen force would have on popular attitudes. "In France as well as in England," he wrote, "only the formation of a national militia raised the military spirit of the nation, and created enthusiasm for fatherland and freedom, which," he added in polite criticism of Prussia, "is not as vigorously evident in other countries."[9] Although regional militias had been raised in the past, they were not highly regarded in the army, and Scharnhorst could hardly have expected a positive response. But as he clarified his own ideas he led his superiors to consider new or formerly rejected possibilities.

Scharnhorst's memorandum, the academy, and the Military Society are instances of scattered efforts before the disaster of 1806 to learn from and respond to the new.[10] New developments in organization, operations, and tactics rarely appear at once but emerge gradually, and individuals gain a sense of their significance and of the need to find answers to them before institutions respond. The academy and the Military Society were too recent to affect operations when war came, but they helped solidify Scharnhorst's position. He impressed his new environment with his mastery of technical matters, which was sharpened rather than diluted by his sensitivity to the larger context. It was Scharnhorst's teaching that set Clausewitz, who called him the father of his mind, on the path of understanding that a general theory of war demands both going beyond war and the reciprocal testing of contemporary evidence against knowledge of the past.

In the campaign of 1806, Scharnhorst was still too junior to make himself heard in the endless councils of war that slowed and confused operations. At Auerstedt, when the Duke of Brunswick sent him to restore the situation on the left flank, he might have objected that this was not the time for him to be away, but he welcomed the opportunity for once to be in control of at least a part of the action. He succeeded, but his absence left the army without unified command after the duke was mortally wounded. In the following weeks Scharnhorst was able to introduce a degree of order in the wild retreat north. After Lübeck was taken he capitulated with Blücher, was soon exchanged, and by January 1807 had made his way to East Prussia.

By this time the Prussian army had been reduced to a junior partner to the stronger but sluggish Russian forces in East Prussia. In addition, it still defended Silesia in the south and the town of Kolberg on the Baltic coast to the west. In these two outlying theaters of operations, relatively junior officers commanded and held the French at bay until the fighting ended in June 1807. Kolberg, surrounded and besieged for months, was defended by Gneisenau, a non-Prussian, his social background only a step or two superior to Scharnhorst's, who had transferred from one of the small German states to the Prussian army; Silesia, by Count Goetzen, member of an old, distinguished family. Both men were inventive and charismatic leaders. Gneisenau rose to be Blücher's chief of staff at Waterloo and eventually reached the rank of field marshal. He became Clausewitz's patron and closest friend. Goetzen, equally brilliant, Scharnhorst's protégé since the days of the Military Society, was ill throughout the war, and his career soon ended. In East Prussia Scharnhorst served as chief of staff of the Prussian contingent, which with a larger Russian force under Bennigsen fought superior French forces to a draw at the Battle of Eylau in February 1807. He impressed the king by his energy and competence at a time of harrowing material and psychic loss, was promoted to major-general, and surprisingly found himself near the center of whatever power still remained.

❋ 3 ❋

While fighting was still in progress, in December 1806, Frederick William from temporary headquarters in Ortelsburg, south of Königsberg, declared his intention to establish a commission to investigate and redress conditions in the army that had led to the disaster. His announcement, the so-called Ortelsburg Publicandum, drafted by the king with strong input from his advisors, preempted some of the commission's tasks by already issuing several new regulations— one being that henceforth other ranks who distinguished themselves could be commissioned "just like a prince"— and by pronouncing punishment on nine officers for having surrendered their commands to the French, among them General von Kleist, a relative of the poet, who had capitulated at Magdeburg with nearly 20,000 effectives. The severity of the punishments suggest that Frederick William, who remained unforgiving in these matters, had a decisive hand in at least that part of the Publicandum. They included one sentence of death, which could not be carried out, the colonel in question having fled the state.

After the defeat at Friedland on June 14, and the conclusion of an armistice, by which time the army had shrunk to one fourth of its original strength, Frederick William returned to his program of investigating the army's conduct and creating a new, more effective force. It was now decided to establish not one but two commissions: in July, a Military Reorganization Commission with Scharnhorst as chairman; in August, a commission to investigate the conduct of every unit and officer in the campaign. To underline the gravity of the investigation and assure the officer corps' acceptance of the outcome, this second body was chaired by two of the king's brothers.[11]

Commissions of enquiry at the end of a war, especially one ending in defeat, are not uncommon. But the investigation's scale and intensity were unprecedented at the time and may not have been equaled since. The commission began work toward the end of 1807 and continued until the summer of 1812. It investigated every surrender and every capitulation of a town or a fortress, together with the operations leading up to these events; demanded detailed reports from every senior commander, commanding officer of independent units, and eventually from every regimental and battalion commander; and ordered each regiment that had been in action to set up tribunals, their findings to be reviewed by the commission, which in turn forwarded recommendations to the king. It also issued or denied certificates of good conduct to officers of the relevant units who were no longer on active service, and who required a certificate for re-employment or to receive a pension. Six generals were killed in the war. Of the 132 generals who survived, not all of whom had seen action, 17 were cashiered, as were 50 field-grade officers out of 851, and 141 captains and subalterns out of 4,057. The percentage of dishonorable dismissals was highest for generals, about 13 percent, and lowest for captains, lieutenants, and ensigns, about 3 percent.[12] The investigations reasserted the authority of monarch and state, and those who survived the process of purification may have received a useful injection of self-assurance at a critical time.

Placing Scharnhorst at the head of the Military Reorganization Commission indicates both the reputation he had gained and the impression the defeats had made on the king.[13] For once Frederick William was shaken loose from his anxious adherence to the accustomed. But he soon recovered and appointed three of his adjutants to the group, men attuned to his views, who together with a fourth conservative officer for a time formed a majority. This changed after two were eased into marginal tasks, and Scharnhorst threatened to resign unless a third was replaced. By the end of 1807, five of the six regular members, among them Gneisenau and Goetzen, favored extensive change. Half of the commission was made up of men of modest social background. Scharnhorst's father, as we know, had begun life as a free peasant, and the title Gneisenau's father had assumed reflected family tradition but could not be documented; a third member was the son of a recently ennobled judge. When Scharnhorst appointed Clausewitz as his aide and chief of his secretariat, yet another officer of educated middle-class descent joined the commission's work. Their background did not automatically turn these men into radical innovators, but it was hardly without influence. Professionally, too, the commission's makeup did not reflect the army's formerly dominant elements—the guards, line infantry, and heavy cavalry. Scharnhorst was a gunner, and two others had served in the light infantry.

French victories caused the commission to be established. But Scharnhorst and his associates aimed at more than Prussian versions of French methods. In their eyes, French strategy and tactics raised general issues, each susceptible to more than one solution. The reforms must be adapted to Prussian conditions, which would have to be adjusted in turn. Learning was more than copying; it should lead to the development of new responses. The commission's agenda and that of its working groups on particular matters eventually covered every aspect of Prussia's military institutions. It submitted recommendations to Frederick William, and defending its proposals against his doubts and the insinuations of his conservative intimates became a major part of the commission's work. Some of the subjects addressed were purely military, the organization of the army, for instance. Other matters, such as manpower sources and the selection of officers, were basically social and political. Many issues—discipline, for one—pertained to both. Consequently the commission had to work in close agreement with the king's chief minister as he reformed the civil administration and introduced greater legal equality in society—first, Baron vom Stein, who for a time attended the commission's meetings; then, after the French forced him from office, Count Hardenberg.

In the last analysis, most changes in the army were dependent on change in the civil realm. The priority of politics and policy over war, which Clausewitz would begin to define some years later, the commission already demonstrated in 1808 and 1809 in the social and institutional spheres. Recruiting, to mention only this, was linked to the discipline to which the rank and file was subject. In turn, discipline affected the army's drill, which determined tactics. Even some supporters of reform did not fully recognize the interdependence of civil and military elements that was always uppermost in Scharnhorst's thinking. As Clausewitz noted in his

Linear tactics, drilled to a high degree of precision and effectiveness, had been the army's touchstone for nearly a century. Fusing thousands of men into a compact force, responsive to a single command, and the discipline and training to bring this about, fit well with the army's concept of itself and of the social structure that determined the place and relationship of officers and rank and file. For many, the Prussian line with its rapid evolutions and volleys was emblematic of the army as a whole. They could reasonably argue that to dilute a system that had often proved itself was a gamble, particularly as the alternative seemed hardly persuasive—men, who had been drilled to move only on command and in unison, who had never been taught to aim their muskets, let alone to think for themselves, were now expected to fight in open order with muskets that were notoriously inaccurate. Beneath these practical concerns lay the conservatives' fear that open order would promote indiscipline in the rank and file, perhaps even revolutionary ideas.

To draft new infantry and cavalry manuals while responding to the critics, Scharnhorst appointed two committees, both of which he chaired. The three members who served with him on the infantry committee were a royal adjutant, to provide the necessary political cover, and two men of bourgeois descent, of whom Clausewitz was one. A survey of manuals of other European armies had already begun, as had experiments with various formations. For an earlier Prussian model with which to quiet the concerns of traditionalists, Scharnhorst chose the army's sole regiment of dismounted chasseurs, or *Fussjäger*, an elite unit armed with rifles and trained to fight in small groups as well as in compact formations. In the last war the regiment had been commanded by Hans David von Yorck, the same officer who in 1812, as commander of the Prussian corps with the *Grande Armée*, was to conclude the Convention of Tauroggen, which initiated Prussia's break with France.

As a twenty-one-year-old subaltern in a Prussian infantry regiment, Yorck had been court-martialed for insubordination and cashiered. He took service with the Dutch East India Company, sailed to the Cape of Good Hope, and may have been present at naval engagements in the East Indies. Back in Prussia he sought readmission to the army, but Frederick the Great repeatedly turned him down. "After your recent naval service," one of the king's letters went, "I must reasonably have doubts about reemploying you in the infantry," adding the royal insult that "it would be the same as if a cook wanted to be a dancing teacher."[14] In the more relaxed atmosphere after Frederick's death, Yorck was taken back, and eleven years later he was given command of the *Fussjäger*. In 1806 he led the regiment in a successful rearguard action, which allowed parts of the defeated army to cross the Elbe. He was wounded, taken prisoner, and exchanged. Like Scharnhorst, he eventually reached East Prussia and was promoted to major-general.

Yorck was a man of aggressive individuality, skeptical of received opinion whether conservative or liberal, and as unreserved in middle age as he had been in his youth. He did not hesitate to lecture a member of the royal family that by reducing distinctions of privilege in society, the prince was endangering his own. He was equally irritated by aristocratic pretensions. When asked of his wife's descent, he silenced his aristocratic questioner with the answer, "Of no descent." His wife, like his mother, did, indeed, come from a modest family. Whatever his rhetoric, which has led historians to contradictory views of his politics,[15] he abolished corporal punishment in his regiment before 1806, forbade the use of the cane at drill, and adjusted his men's tactics to the French model. He already chaired a committee on revising training instructions when Scharnhorst asked his help in drafting the manual. Yorck had a month's seniority in rank over Scharnhorst and could not serve under him, but he acted as advisor to the working group, and the new infantry regulations were based in part on the instructions he had drafted for his regiment. The manuals were adopted early in 1812. By then the Reorganization Commission had issued new articles of war, which eliminated corporal punishment in the army. "Mild treatment," it declared, would suffice to assure order and discipline.

As noted earlier, conservatives feared that skirmishing and the abolition of the cane would weaken discipline. Later some even asserted that their introduction led to Yorck's insubordination in December 1812, when he withdrew the Prussian force he commanded from the *Grande Armée*, after which, again without orders, he encouraged the East Prussian estates to mobilize their militia, prohibited under the

Convention of Paris—two unauthorized acts that amounted to a Prussian declaration of independence from France. But rather than blaming skirmishing for Yorck's disobedience, it is more probable that a man of known independence of judgment, eager to break with France, decided to act when he saw the extent of Napoleon's disaster more clearly from his post in western Russia than one could in Berlin.

The new infantry manual prescribed simple combinations of open and closed evolutions in concise terms that avoided formality and emphasized individual initiative. Much the same may be said of the new cavalry regulations. The infantry manual was only one-third the length of, respectively, the French *Ordonnance* of 1791, the basis of French infantry tactics during the revolution and empire, the British *Rules and Regulations*, and the Austrian manual of 1807. Its 131 pages covered most of the matter for which the Prussian infantry regulations of 1788 required 546.[16] The difference in content between the two Prussian manuals, issued only twenty-five years apart—between the complexity and length of the one and the clarity and brevity of the other—is a fair symbol of the commission's achievements in the exclusively or largely military sphere.

⊠ 4 ⊠

Issuing new manuals was an important step. Among others taken by the commission were the establishment of a Ministry of War, which brought together separate and often competing agencies. The organization of the army was at last freed from its former fragmentation by combining battalions and regiments into permanent brigades. Beginnings were made to create a general staff, and a war college was founded to raise the educational level of officers, help them understand the army beyond the narrow confines of their unit and branch of service, and gradually introduce a common conception of operations. The position of inspector-general for the light service was created, to which Yorck was appointed. Regulations for more realistic maneuvers and exercises were issued, and a commission was set up to oversee musketry, skirmishing, and field exercises. Another body reviewed the regulations for the manufacture of arms and equipment, and the building of fortifications. A corps of engineers and a military police corps were established, medical and hospital services were placed on a permanent basis, and, to correct a major failure of the old system, supply and transport were taken out of the hands of private contractors and made the responsibility of new supply and transport battalions, although for the time being these units existed only on paper.

These changes affected matters that were largely or wholly military, but all had social and economic implications. Of a different order, and far more directly engaged with society, whether elites or the population at large, was the problem of manpower: who was to serve, and under what conditions. Linked to this basic issue were two others: the question of discipline and military justice, which the commission answered by eliminating corporal punishment and issuing new articles of war that brought the military code to closer agreement to the civil code, and, second, the selection and promotion of officers.

As mentioned earlier, the army drew its men from two sources: first, foreign mercenaries, primarily from other German states, but also from the Low Countries, Switzerland, Alsace, and Eastern Europe. In the last years before the war, foreigners made up between one-third and one-half of the rank and file.[17] In 1802 their number amounted to some 80,500 men. Natives not freed from serving were the second source, mainly the sons of serfs, day-laborers, small craftsmen, and men sentenced for minor crimes. Exempt were the nobility (although it was expected that many able-bodied sons of noble parents entered the service directly or by way of a cadet school), almost all of the bourgeoisie, Jews as of 1799, Mennonites somewhat earlier, and residents of Berlin, of some other towns, and of a number of privileged districts and territories. It was only a slight exaggeration for Yorck to declare that anyone not a beggar or vagabond was exempt.[18] The country was divided into recruitment districts, each assigned to a military unit, which drew the men needed from those available. This system, introduced in the 1730s against much noble opposition, weakened the control of the landowner over his serfs, who now answered to a higher authority, so that the state extended its reach over its most privileged subjects even as it gained cheap recruits. Until 1792, when the length of service was reduced to twenty years, men served in the ranks until disability or death. In peacetime actual service was limited to three months a year for natives, a period gradually reduced to six weeks. The rest of the time the men worked as laborers, craftsmen, or in the fields. During this period they were not paid, and some of the savings benefited their commanding officers—a traditional right, which the commission was quick to abolish.

These policies, deeply embedded in the social structure, were now scrapped, as the government's freeing of the serfs, the removal or reduction of obligations owed by some and privileges possessed by others, brought society closer to legal equality. The state's financial ruin, and the political intentions of the civilian and military leaders of the reform program, pointed to the introduction of general conscription, which imposed an equal duty on males of all classes, even if certain groups could perform this duty under more favorable conditions—for example, the sons of officers and officials had access to cadet schools, from which they entered the army at a higher level than did common recruits.[19] As we know, Scharnhorst and many others with him believed that military duties, universally shared, would generate ideals of citizenship and patriotism and help turn the state into a nation. The *levée en masse* of the French Revolution served as the political-military model, but without the French conscript's right of 1793 to furnish a substitute if he had the money, a right again confirmed under the Directory.

Opposition to general conscription came from many quarters. Previously exempt cities and towns protested, but so did liberal supporters of other reforms. Famous is a statement by a senior official, Stein's advisor on constitutional questions, in a memorandum sent to Stein in September 1808, in which the writer declared he would resign if the concept of universal military obligation, which he thought degraded the individual to a simple means to an end, became law. "Conscription," he wrote, "is the grave of all culture, of science and industry, of the citizen's freedom, and of all human happiness."[20] His concern was premature, for as he was writing the peace treaty with France was signed, which restricted the size of the Prussian army, so that the issue of conscription for the time being became irrelevant. But administrative preparations for the future continued, and when the law establishing conscription was at last signed in February 1813, first for the duration of the war, then in permanence, it was implemented with only sporadic difficulties.

To increase the army's strength beyond the limits imposed by France, the commission introduced a program of secretly training as many as fifteen men over strength in each company. After several months of basic drill they were given indefinite leave back to civilian life, to return to the colors when called. Until 1812 about 40,000 men had gone through the process, almost doubling the army, though the number still fell far short of the demands in the final campaigns against Napoleon.

On the assumption that the obligation of military service would eventually extend across the whole of society,

Scharnhorst and his associates planned for an expansive future armed force: the reformed standing army was to be joined by a militia, eventually named *Landwehr*, a term that closely translates "National Guard." The army and Landwehr were to be supported by a home guard and others with rudimentary training, serving close to home, the *Landsturm*. Finally, the population at large was to be organized and armed to resist enemy occupation.

Uprisings in the Vendée, the Tyrol, and Spain provided examples for making irregular war a component of state policy. In two courses at the new War College, Clausewitz lectured on the war of detachments, raids, and ambushes, the so-called little war, its relation with conventional operations on the one hand, and guerrilla warfare on the other. First steps were taken to cover the state with a network of officials, retired soldiers, and others, to act as local commanders and maintain links with the regular forces. In the end, neither insurrection nor the Landsturm, which with some justice might be termed "organized insurrection," became reality.[21] But as the logical conclusion of a continuum—from volunteer to universal conscription, to the *levée en masse*, to the armed people opposing the invader—insurrection and the Landsturm stimulated Scharnhorst's thinking and that of his closest followers. They associated the idealized image of the partisan with patriotism, initiative, and self-reliance, and they strove to introduce these qualities into conventional formations, so far as that was possible. But few believed that large insurrections could succeed in Northern Europe. They always planned to oppose Napoleon with regular forces, albeit of a new dynamic and flexibility.[22]

The first part of Scharnhorst's plans for the army's future structure—the combination of standing army and national guard—was implemented in 1813, but not in the form originally intended. Scharnhorst thought of the Landwehr as a force of the people, co-equal with the regular army, and largely autonomous in its organization. It was to be made up of civilians with some military training, who, subject to royal confirmation, elected their own officers up to the rank of captain. In times of peace, educational qualifications were prerequisite for election—which limited commissions to individuals with some economic resources. In wartime, bravery and ability sufficed. Officers were to have the same privileges as their comrades in the standing army. This was truly revolutionary: it had not been Prussian practice to arm civilians and let them choose their own leaders, who would be co-opted in the state's military elite. With these proposals Scharnhorst hoped to make the force attractive to the bourgeoisie—and it is important to recognize that he was less concerned about forms of government than about making society legally more equal, and reducing social barriers to commissions and advancement. His aim was to rest the state's armed power on a unity of government, the old elites, and the middle range of society, into which men from below would have easier access.

The opposition his efforts encountered changed their outcome, and when the Landwehr was formed early in 1813—to reach a strength of 120,000 men by year's end—it was no longer the largely self-sufficient bourgeois force that Scharnhorst had envisioned, first steps in a process that by the 1820s made it fully subordinate to the standing army—a development motivated by the need to maintain standards of training and discipline, but even more so by conservative dislike of the Landwehr's privileges and their social implications.

To an extent, Scharnhorst's hopes for the Landwehr were realized by the improvised creation in February 1813 of detachments of chasseurs or *Jäger*, made up of volunteers between seventeen and twenty-two years old, who could pay for their uniforms and mounts. After some months of service attached to regular units, they could elect their own officers, subject to royal confirmation, and could also fill vacant slots for officers in the army and Landwehr. By the summer of 1813 they numbered close to 8,500 men.[23] They were employed mainly on patrols, outposts, and other duties of light troops. After the war their retired members played an important role in society, culture, and politics. They extended military status to the bourgeoisie—though not on as broad a scale as Scharnhorst had envisaged—and, as became evident in the following generation, were a force in the gradual militarization of north German society.

◼ 5 ◼

Before 1813 the expansion of the army, in whatever form, could only be discussed, not yet carried out; but other innovations were not dependent on French approval. Politically and socially the most significant and difficult of these was the issue of who could be an officer. In the Ortelsburg Publicandum Frederick William had declared that, for the duration of the war, any deserving sergeant and private soldier, regardless of family background, could be commissioned. Gneisenau and Goetzen, who in their commands in Kolberg and Silesia had enjoyed a degree of autonomy, made such promotions—steps that strengthened the morale of their forces—but after the war were widely criticized. That did not keep the Reorganization Commission from following their example. Regulations issued in June 1808 put the appointment of officers in the regular army on a new basis. A title of nobility had been almost required for a commission—almost because even when after the Seven Years' War the army dismissed untitled officers or officers unable to document their title, Clausewitz's father among them, a fair number remained in the artillery, the technical services, and the light cavalry. In 1806 perhaps one-tenth of the officers on active and garrison duty did not carry a title of nobility.[24] The total of bourgeois or lower-class descent would be far higher if men with dubious titles and those raised to the nobility in the course of their career were included. Now examinations replaced nobility as a qualification for appointment or promotion to ensign and lieutenant. The successful candidate still required the approval of his comrades and the monarch. Under the new regulations, the subalterns of a regiment with an opening for a lieutenant nominated three of the regiment's ensigns who had passed the qualifying exam. After a second examination, the captains chose one name to submit to the king.[25] In later years this compromise between the new principle of legal equality, the peer group's social influence, and royal power took other forms; but in the Prussian army up to the First World War, a unit's officers voted on qualified candidates, which in practice narrowed rather than broadened the officer corps' social character.

The Reorganization Commission not only opened access to commissions; by reducing the power of seniority, it changed the officers' conditions of service. Seniority still determined promotion to the rank of major, after which their superiors controlled further promotion and assignments. The former practice of assigning generals to particular duties according to seniority—which helps explain the advanced age of some commanding generals in 1806—was also modified.

Taken together, these innovations created an army that in its organization and manner was largely new. It met the operational and tactical challenges posed by the armies of the French Republic and institutionalized under Napoleon. If between 1813 and 1815 the Prussian high command could not equal the emperor's strategic brilliance, its strategy, unlike his, was in accord with the geographic and political facts and could call on the required manpower and resources.

The armies of the other major powers also learned to deal with what was new in the opponent they faced. They, too, saw the new through the lens of existing conditions and attitudes, a lens that clarified some matters but obscured others. Each army made changes. These differed somewhat in tactics and administration, and considerably in respect to discipline and the appointment and training of officers. Everywhere, too, changes in the structure and functioning of the armed forces were affected by developments in society, economy, and politics, and in turn affected them. But no other army had been defeated as severely as the Prussian, and in response no army broke as quickly with the past, nor perhaps as sharply. That, together with the intensely restrictive character of Prussian absolutism, and the determination of the leaders of the reforms to remove or weaken many of its policies and methods, led to innovations of unusual magnitude.

The Military Reorganization Commission generally succeeded in changing matters that were largely or wholly military: organization, administration, the education of officers, tactical and operational doctrine. It succeeded in part, and in part it failed to achieve equality of opportunity in the military. Turning the regular army into an institution more closely linked with all segments of the population meant essentially expanding the obligation of military service, and changing its motivation. Service to the nation became the new appeal, but the old authoritarian system remained, only now with an added justification. Scharnhorst's effort to integrate the bourgeoisie not only into the army but into the officer corps was watered down. That raises the question whether he could have prevented this development; but at the beginning of the war of 1813, when he served both as de facto minister of war and as the army's chief of staff—a mark of the exceptional impact this newcomer had made on state and army—he was wounded in the Battle of Grossgörschen, and at the age of fifty-seven died of his wound. The state did not keep the bargain he had proposed: subjects become citizens; citizens defend their country. Nor did Frederick William fulfill his promise of 1814 to grant a constitution, a failure that was to have large consequences in German history. When peace returned, Scharnhorst's followers were politically neutralized—some being awarded marks of great distinction as they were pushed aside—and not even Scharnhorst could have halted the return of old political and social attitudes. The victories over Napoleon between 1813 and 1815, which validated Scharnhorst's reforms and restored the power of the Prussian state, also restored the power of Prussian conservatism, which had never ceased to resist some reforms and bend others to its own advantage.

4

The Conquest of Reality by Theory

The first part of this study traced the war of 1806, which challenged the defeated to understand the reasons for their defeat and adopt more effective methods for a future conflict. The next two chapters addressed cultural and social forces that influenced the response and help explain it, and the response itself, which took the form of institutional and individual action in conflicts that ranged innovation against current policy and tradition. Each of these events was unique, yet developments similar to them occur throughout history: battles are won and lost; artists and writers re-create war in their works, though not all wars lead to great aesthetic achievements; institutions strive to adjust and respond to defeats—all specifics that are typical phenomena. In that regard the topic to which we now turn differs. After a war, individuals generally analyze what has occurred and offer their interpretations. But it is rare for their ideas and formulations to transcend the immediate situation. Some of the pragmatic responses to the problems raised in 1806, on the other hand, became steps toward an understanding of war in its totality, war as such.

That understanding built on earlier efforts to reach beyond particulars to broader interpretations. The two decades before and after 1806 saw the publication of many theoretical studies of war. "Theoretical study" is a vague term. At the time it was applied to books and articles that by reason of their general statements differed from campaign narrative, military memoirs, and biographies. Even today, the intent to generalize is often taken for theory, no matter how the generalizations are arrived at—raising questions to which we shall return. In the last years before the French Revolution, important works had appeared that not only dealt with issues of organization, tactics, and strategy—all widely discussed—but addressed the place of armed forces in society in such books as *Le Soldat-Citoyen* by Servan de Gerby, the future Girondin minister of war. The revolution added impetus to the more general studies of civil–military relations, as well as to books and articles on specifically military, often technical, issues. Debates in the National Assembly and the Convention led to further publications in France and elsewhere, as, increasingly, did the wars of the revolution and French expansion.

Of this body of literature, the writings that eventually had the strongest resonance were those of Jomini and Clausewitz. Each man began to publish before the war of 1806, in which both served. Even before the events of that year blended with Jomini's experiences in subsequent wars, they confirmed him in ideas he was developing. For Clausewitz the catastrophic outcome for Prussia was not only an intellectual challenge but a psychological shock. For both, the war became a source of issues that occupied and advanced their broader analyses. Directly and indirectly, the year 1806 remained a presence in their writings on the timelessness of war.

Clausewitz's early essays and his later historical and theoretical manuscripts are grounded in his encounter with the new in war before and during the fall campaign of 1806. They are among the Prussian and German responses that are the subjects of this study; but obviously they are also more than that. Just as conscription and new infantry tactics have earlier roots, a subsequent history, and yet belong to our theme, so do Clausewitz's theoretical writings. The aim of these texts, their method and content, will, I hope, emerge more clearly if they are examined in conjunction with some of Jomini's work and with that of another analyst of modern war, Heinrich Dietrich von Bülow, whose ideas stimulated both Jomini and Clausewitz, although not in ways he would have wished.

Taking note of these writers also adds to our understanding of the environment in which they grew up, and that influenced their work. Clausewitz spent his first twenty-six years, half of his life, in the military world of late-Enlightenment, precatastrophe Prussia. The drama and poetry of the time, as well as Kant's critical examination of the issues of reality and perception and its echoes in works of popularization, strongly influenced him. The development of Clausewitz's ideas owes much to the concepts and methods he found in these writings, which he tested against his experiences as a soldier and expanded beyond the immediate present with the help of historical studies that even in his youth were unusually extensive. He encountered and probed serious analyses of war in the writings of a number of contemporary theorists, among whom Scharnhorst, above all, widened his perspective. After contrasting the aim of his theoretical work with that of Bülow and Jomini, I want to discuss Clausewitz's conception of theory, outline some of its salient elements, and consider his readers' reactions. To conclude, it will be useful to return once more to the reflection of war in art and literature, and suggest some links between the aesthetic theories of the time and Clausewitz's development of a theoretical understanding of war.

It is not unusual to compare Jomini's and Clausewitz's ideas. The comparisons often have a combative subtext, sometimes barely hidden, that treats the two writers as competitors in an intellectual contest.[1] That they began to examine war analytically around the same time need not, of course, make them competitors. Nor does the criticism each leveled at the other's work. Competition in the usual sense was hardly possible since Clausewitz published little in his life, and Jomini reacted largely, if not entirely, to his posthumous publications. The idea of rivalry seems rather to have originated in the minds of their readers, some of whom even today assume that using arguments of the one as a stick with which to beat the other takes the place of interpretation. In the process they ignore, among much else, measures of agreement between the two. Here I do not intend to argue for one over the other. Jomini's bibliography with the many revisions of his texts is in any case too complex and Clausewitz's work too extensive to compare in a brief discussion. But taking note of some of Jomini's arguments and conclusions may bring out the contours and substance of Clausewitz's ideas with greater clarity.

◼ I ◼

In their studies of war, both Jomini and Clausewitz responded to great historical and personal challenges. Jomini, born in March 1779 in Payerne in the Territory of Vaud in French-speaking Switzerland, where his father held positions in local government, attended schools in Payerne and Aarau, and at the age of seventeen, by which time he was already interested in military affairs, became a clerk in a Swiss bank in Paris.[2] Less than two years later he returned to Payerne, where civil unrest had broken out, which opened the door to French intervention. He was appointed a junior officer in the local militia and soon became aide de camp to the minister of war of the new Helvetic Republic. In 1799 he was promoted to captain, and the following year, after French forces defeated the Austro-Russian intervention in Switzerland, to *chef de bataillon* in the Swiss army. At the age of twenty-one, without having yet seen action, his connections, administrative abilities, political intelligence, and outgoing, evidently engaging personality had raised him to a rank equivalent to that of major or lieutenant colonel. He was well on his way to his true calling: to understand—which to him meant codify—the wars the revolution had unleashed.

As Jomini was advancing and achieving some prominence in the Franco-Swiss military world, Clausewitz, born a year later than Jomini, in July 1780, was an obscure second lieutenant in the Prussian army.[3] He came from a family of Lutheran pastors. His father was a retired lieutenant, now an internal revenue official, his grandfather professor of theology at the University of Halle, whose widow married as her second husband the commanding officer of the Prussian 34th infantry regiment, which led to Clausewitz's appointment as lance corporal in this regiment shortly before his twelfth birthday. Between the first months of 1793 and the spring of 1795, during which time he was promoted to ensign and in his fifteenth year to second lieutenant, the regiment served along the Rhine and in Alsace against the armies of revolutionary France. Clausewitz saw much infantry combat on the company and battalion level. In these years the regimental diary records participation in three victorious battles, fourteen engagements, of which nine were declared successes, three assaults on defended positions, one siege, and one cannonade.[4] Six years of garrison service followed in a regiment with one of the best regimental schools in the army. In 1801 Clausewitz was in the first group of officers to gain admission to Scharnhorst's Institute for Young Officers, which opened a new intellectual world to him. When he left the institute in 1804 at the head of his class, he was appointed adjutant of Prince August of Prussia, a nephew of the king, in whose grenadier battalion he was to serve in the war of 1806.

In 1800 Jomini published his first articles, two brief pieces, one on diplomatic issues, the other a discussion of forms of government, which gave preference to the limited form of democracy, dominated by regional elites, in which he had grown up. The following year he resigned his commission and returned to Paris where he worked for a military supplier. In his free time he read military history and theory and began to write a study that contrasted the Seven Years' War with Napoleon's recent campaigns in Italy. In his reading he found the somewhat conflicting histories of the Seven Years' War of Henry Lloyd and Georg Friedrich von Tempelhof, together with Bülow's recently published reflections on modern war, particularly stimulating. Bülow's comparison of Frederick the Great's campaigns with those of Napoleon suggested similarities to Jomini, which in turn led him to speculate on the possibility of developing strategic truths that rose above temporal differences in organization and weapons. Reading Bülow stimulated him to search for and define universal principles.

As is often the case with transitional thinkers, Bülow's ideas on war combined insights and blindness.[5] He saw that a revolution of war was under way and, as mentioned earlier, predicted that future wars would be decided by skirmishers—an implied rejection of the automatic obedience to which he had been subject, and which he had imposed, during his service in the Prussian army. Bülow recognized that new concepts and terms were needed to facilitate the serious study of war. Some terms he suggested are still in use today—his lasting contribution to the literature on war. But he failed to understand how greatly political and social changes of the 1790s had increased the potential of mobility and battle. Instead, his thinking remained bound by rationalist analysis. He favored maneuver over battle and put forward the theory that the success of a military operation was largely determined by the geometric relationship of its base to its geographic objective. Jomini accepted Bülow's belief in general principles but replaced Bülow's principles with his own.

In 1804 Jomini approached one of the great figures of the new French empire, Marshal Ney, probably already a slight acquaintance, and requested financial support for the publication of the first two volumes of his *Traité de grande tactique*. Ney not only provided the funds—the two volumes were soon published—he appointed Jomini a "volunteer aide de camp," in which capacity Jomini was present at the battles of Elchingen and Ulm. The following year his position was regularized by promotion to colonel, seconded to the staff— a remarkably rapid advancement. In September 1806 he was appointed first adjutant to Ney, and he served under Ney both at the Battle of Jena and the following year at the Battle of Eylau. In the interval, in December 1806, he published a summary of his principal concepts under the title *Résumé des principes généraux de l'art de la guerre*.[6] Separately and as the concluding thirty-fifth chapter of the third volume of his *Treatise*, the *Résumé* became the most influential of his writings. It opens with the firm pronouncement that "at all times there have been fundamental principles on which good results in warfare depend ... these principles are immutable, independent of types of weapon, time, and country." By "warfare" Jomini here means conventional war. Civil and religious wars he rejects as "wars of opinion," which, he believes, makes them ill suited to rigorous analysis—an exclusion that says a great deal about his conception of the subject.[7] Genius and experience, he adds, "indicate the different ways in which [these principles] can be used"—a further important qualification, which does not, however, reduce his claim of defining absolute military truths.[8]

According to Jomini, the fundamental strategic principle to be followed if possible in all conventional wars is that of operating along interior lines, striking at parts of the opposing force, as Frederick in the Seven Years' War turned first on one then on another of the armies moving against him from east, south, and west. This basic strategic key Jomini combines with a second principle, borrowed from Frederick's maneuver at Leuthen, that of "bringing superior force to bear on a point where the enemy is both weaker and liable to crippling damage."[9] It is again indicative of his way of thinking that he uses a tactical measure—one army's action in a battle—as a model for strategy, that is, action by various forces on a large scale. Unlike Bülow, he recognizes the dynamics of Napoleonic warfare but does his best to reduce them to a formula. In place of Bülow's argument that success in war is determined by the static concept of the relationship of base to objective, Jomini claims general validity for an advance on interior lines, followed by an attack with massive force against a decisive point. He was to insist on the supreme correctness of this combination for the remaining sixty-six years of his life. A strategic leitmotif, it runs through all of his writings.

◨ 2 ◨

In 1805, the year the first volumes of Jomini's *Treatise* appeared, Clausewitz published his first article—a review written a year earlier of Bülow's latest work, which Scharnhorst helped him place in the most important German military journal.[10] Jomini agreed with Bülow's approach but disagreed with his conclusions. Clausewitz's objections are more basic. They document an early stage in his effort to create "scientific" certitude for his own analysis of war and furthermore demonstrate the remarkable consistency that runs through his work, from its beginning to his last notes—not in each of the conclusions he draws, which evolve on the basis of experience and study, but in a rare concern for the methodological soundness with which he formulates and develops his arguments.[11] He rejects Bülow's work on three main grounds. Above all, he writes, Bülow's method is flawed. His definitions and conclusions are derived from observations; but observations that are not backed by hypotheses are matters of chance, which work against valid generalizations. Bülow's treatment of strategy and tactics, based on what he has experienced and read, is a case in point. He defines strategy as "all military movements out of the enemy's cannon range or range of vision," and tactics as "all movements within this range." Very well, Clausewitz responds, but how do these definitions accommodate technological change, and why do they say nothing about the purpose of the concepts defined? In their place Clausewitz proposes definitions that are not only different, but different in kind: "Tactics constitute the theory of the use of armed forces in battle; strategy constitutes the theory of using battle for the purposes of the war"—the term "use" incorporating "threat of use." Rather than descriptive, Clausewitz's definitions—then and later— are functional; they take account of means and end in war and are applicable at all times and to every conceivable type of armed conflict, from war between regular forces to armed uprisings, guerrilla warfare, or terror campaigns.

Clausewitz's second criticism of Bülow is that his theories are unrealistic. They are based on geography and mathematics but ignore the actions of the enemy and the physical and psychological effects of the fighting. Strategy, however, Clausewitz objects, "is nothing without battle [or the threat of battle]." Furthermore, and that is his third point, any meaningful theory of war must address not only elements susceptible to mathematical analysis, such as distances and angles of approach, but also imponderables—the commander's psychology, the morale of the troops, and above all the political aims of the belligerents.

Jomini has been subjected to similar criticism even by some who otherwise find much of value in his writings.

In his previously cited work, Jean-Jacques Langendorf goes so far as to observe that Jomini lacks "the dialectical sense of war."[12] It is an odd failing in an analyst of conflict; but the believer in a strategic system based on a fixed pattern of action, even if circumstances are to govern how they are employed, is not likely to pay much attention to opposing capacities and plans.

In notes on strategy that Clausewitz wrote in 1808 and 1809, he found much good sense in the principles that Jomini substituted for Bülow's theory—the use of interior lines, massing one's forces against a vulnerable target—which was not the same as admitting their general validity. Jomini, he writes, "reasons and demonstrates far more solidly [than Bülow]; but to determine the value of his abstractions we should seriously ask ourselves whether we would exchange the whole of Frederick's life as commander of armies for these few general and easily understood statements. . . . I don't believe that Jomini states anything that is actually wrong, but often he presents a happenstance [*etwas Zufälliges*] as something that is fundamental."[13] Clausewitz's criticism, in short, is driven by two related objections: Jomini tries to create a strategic system made up of abstract principles, which cannot meet the infinite variety of possibilities of real life; and Jomini's discussion of strategy is drawn too narrowly. This points to a fundamental characteristic of Clausewitz's thinking. In his youth, when Jomini's *Treatise* first appeared, and later on, Clausewitz certainly gave much thought to strategic and operational matters; but even when he helped develop the army's new infantry tactics during the years of reform and lectured on irregular warfare, his interest kept moving from the tactical and operational specifics to what these particulars might indicate about the larger context, about war itself. In turn, the context in which the military act occurred and the dynamic interaction between opponents—their dialectic—shaped strategy. It was not only Jomini's conclusions, but his method, and above all his narrow conception of strategy as subject to timeless "principles"—that is, rules—that Clausewitz found inadequate.

Bülow and Jomini posed the problem of how to schematize the great variety of military actions. Even as a young lieutenant Clausewitz asked not only *how*, but whether it could be done. His earliest surviving notes, written before he was twenty-five, show that even then he was dissatisfied with contemporary military theorists, finding fault with the methods of their arguments as much as with their conclusions. In an essay of that time on "The Theory of the Art of War Today," he objects that it is not enough to string experiences together and deduce principles from them. Experience, though invaluable, is also fragmentary, even when given an added dimension by material drawn from history. A subheading of the same essay sounds a clear note of impatience with claims that this or that writer had discovered the keys to strategic success: "Whatever great achievements have occurred in the history of war, they were not due to books."[14]

The relationship of theory to reality, which challenged the most creative minds of his generation, was to occupy Clausewitz throughout his life. By taking war out of its military isolation and embedding it in society and politics, he made possible the kind of broad analysis that alone, he thought, might lead to truth, although enlarging its range also expanded its difficulty. The broader view gave him the perspective to identify the components of war, expose them to enquiry, which he tried to make "scientific," and probe their interaction. In a note written probably in his twenties, he defines the scientific treatment of phenomena such as war as "a collection of recognitions [*Erkenntnisse*] organized ... systematically."[15] Later, in one of the four notes commonly printed at the head of *On War*, he is more explicit: the scientific character of his work, he writes, "consists in an attempt to investigate the essence of the phenomena of war and to indicate the links between [them]. No logical conclusion has been avoided; but whenever the thread became too thin I have preferred to break it off and go back to the relevant phenomena of experience"— which explains the many historical examples in *On War*.[16]

To pursue the exploration of Clausewitz's intentions and the manner in which he planned to achieve his goals, we need to consider not only *On War* itself, but also his other writings, in particular the four notes that have appeared at the beginning of *On War* ever since its first publication in 1832, as volumes 1 to 3 of his posthumous works. The first of these notes, "Author's Preface," includes Clausewitz's explanation of the scientific character of his work, cited above. He seems to have written this preface between 1816 and 1818 for a manuscript he describes as consisting of "compressed"

scholars to assert that *On War* in its present state is complete, and to question the notes' relevance, the most recent being Jon Tetsuro Sumida.[20] But not only can the argument not be proved, it is hollow. To refer to *On War* as unfinished is not saying that the work in its present state distorts those of Clausewitz's thoughts that he wanted but could not include in his manuscript. Nothing in the notes suggests that Clausewitz had changed or was changing his mind on major issues. On the contrary, in 1827 he states that in his revisions he intends to place greater emphasis on what he has already written: on the two kinds of war—those that seek to destroy the enemy or make him defenseless, and those with limited goals—as well as to reassert throughout "that *war is nothing but the continuation of policy with other means*" (his emphasis). In reading *On War* it is not difficult, on the basis of what the work already contains, to keep the political nature of war and the two kinds of war foremost in mind. Further revision might have led to more uniform treatment of the various parts of the book; perhaps to the elimination of historical comments that might be interpreted as advocacy where none was intended, and to expanded discussions of the concept of escalation or of some other element in Clausewitz's structural analysis. But none of these matters affects the core of the work. *On War* is not the only achievement in the sciences or the arts that its creator could not complete to the last intended detail, and that is great nevertheless.

If the notes' bearing on *On War* as we know it may raise questions as to the extent of the revisions that Clausewitz actually made, they assuredly are invaluable in casting further light on his purpose and on his method. They confirm that he is writing to understand war, not to establish a doctrine for engaging in it. They emphasize his interest in methods of analytic, "scientific" reasoning. And they underline the continuity and consistency of this basic element in his thought since the days when, as a fifteen-year-old returning to Germany from his first campaigns, he began to read philosophical texts, which, as he later wrote, transformed "the vanity of the little soldier . . . into extreme philosophic ambition."[21]

What does Clausewitz mean when in the first of these notes he writes that he attempts to investigate "the essence of a phenomenon"? To Clausewitz this phrase—which expresses a central philosophic concern—signifies the use of ideal concepts to measure reality. An example: war is distinguished from other activities by the fact of mass violence organized by a political authority (whether legal or illegal, the head of a Stone Age tribe or the leaders of a parliamentary democracy). Absolute violence is unadulterated war—the ideal against which real wars can be measured and interpreted. By thinking through the character and purpose of each element of war in this manner, by finding its "regulative idea," Clausewitz renders it subject to analysis—either to further the development of his argument or to refute it—both being in the spirit of his work.

Observation of events, expanded by historical comparisons and subjected to logical analysis—what is the purpose of a particular element in war, how does it differ from others—makes immanent the "regulative idea" of each. Like Jomini, Clausewitz draws on history to construct his theory. But their concepts of history differ. Jomini traces military actions with little concern for the times in which they occur. He discovers strategic similarities in the wars of Frederick the Great and of Napoleon, which leads him to his principles of war. Clausewitz compares the two men as well, not only in his studies, but in his life. He served in the army that embodied the Frederician tradition, was destroyed by Napoleon, and then tried to reshape itself. The difference between Frederician and Napoleonic warfare was seared in his being. But where Jomini sees strategic similarities, Clausewitz above all sees contextual differences—in the kinds of armies the two men led, in the political worlds in which they lived and which they shaped, in the impact of their background and personalities on their actions. The situation and environment of each man were unique, which means to Clausewitz that the singularity of each era must be part of the analysis of their wars as of all wars. Only by taking account of the differences can we isolate whatever generalities exist, the permanent elements of war—not so much strategy, which must always meet particular conditions, although some common-sense realities generally apply—but such processes as escalation, friction, the relationship of means and end. Clausewitz's recognition of the individuality of each phase of the past, to which his theory responded, also informed his historical studies and writings and turned him into an early practitioner of what soon came to be called "historicism."[22]

☒ 3 ☒

In its ultimate state, Clausewitz's structural analysis is based on identifying the major elements of war, appraising their nature and their relationships, and on recognizing two forces that determine their effectiveness: the opponents' interaction and, in each belligerent, the relationship of means, end, and goal. Means are the armed forces and their actions; end is the political intention; goal the strategic objective that makes the political intention attainable—or on a lower, wholly military level, the operational objective, the attainment of which helps achieve the strategic intention.

These abstractions gain concreteness when we note the major topics of *On War* and the manner in which they are treated.[23] The work's general subject is conventional war; but Clausewitz's definitions encompass all types of armed conflict, and he includes an important chapter on "The People in Arms." The opening chapter—the only one he is on record as regarding definitive out of 127 chapters, some of which, to be sure, are no more than a page in length—begins with the nature of war and the many forms war may take: "War . . . is an act of force to compel our enemy to do our will." In the abstract, there is no limit to the application of that force, and even in reality belligerents may feel pressed to outdo each other, leading to an escalation of violence. But a move from abstraction to the real world may also encounter modifications. War is politically motivated. "The more powerful the motives for war . . . the closer will war approach its abstract concept . . . ; the less intense the motives . . ." the more will war be diverted from its "natural [violent] course." Clausewitz concludes the chapter by outlining three basic conditions that together make up war: "As a total phenomenon," he writes, "its dominant tendencies always make war a remarkable trinity—composed of primordial violence, hatred, and enmity, which are to be regarded as a blind natural force; of the play of chance and probability within which the creative spirit is free to roam; and of its . . . subordination, as an instrument of policy, which makes it subject to reason alone."[24] His conception of war as a composite of three interacting and often conflicting parts creates a new way of seeing war, and a new program for its theoretical analysis.

Discussions follow on the relationship of theory to reality; on the interaction of politics and war, which leads to the proposition that there are two types of war—wars approaching totality, and those with limited means and limited ends; on the significance of psychological factors in society, military forces, and commanders; and finally on the constants of uncertainty and chance, and the difficulties and misunderstandings that are always present when individuals act together, which Clausewitz subsumes under the concept of "friction." The newly significant phenomenon of the people in arms, of irregular warfare, is recognized as "a broadening and intensification of the fermentation process known as war,"[25] and a reciprocal relationship of defense and attack is developed, defense being defined as the stronger form of fighting with the negative purpose; attack as the weaker form with the positive purpose. Every attack is said to lose impetus as it progresses, until a culminating point is reached, after which the attack becomes defense—an enormously contentious proposition that has the great value of forcing us to think about both attack and defense in new ways. These and other general statements are supplemented by more detailed operational propositions that Clausewitz regards as obvious truths, and which theory must find ways to interpret—for example, major successes help bring about minor ones, so that strategic results can be traced back to turning points, or "victory consists not only in the occupation of the battle-field, but in the destruction of the enemy's physical and psychic forces, which is usually not attained until the enemy is pursued after a victorious battle"—a conclusion replete with the echoes of Jena and Auerstedt.[26]

We see that *On War* addresses basic components of war, such as the use of violent force, motives for war, and the political nature of war; constant elements that are difficult to quantify, such as accidents, chance, friction, and psychological factors; but also strategic and operational elements; observations on the dual nature of war—wars fought for major motives with major means, and those fought with limited means for limited ends—the escalating or limiting interaction of opponents; the essence of attack and defense; and even specific operational propositions, for instance "a turning movement can only be justified by general superiority or by having better lines of communication or retreat than the enemy's."[27] In the revisions Clausewitz intended but may only have begun, he planned, as we know, to bring out the two types of war more clearly at every point, and to emphasize throughout his analysis the political nature of war.[28]

Early on, he came to distinguish three types of theory, a distinction often made at the time: utilitarian or prescriptive, pedagogic, and cognitive.[29] The aim of the first type is to improve the effectiveness of action. That was the principal, frequently the only, aim of contemporary military theorists, but Clausewitz found their methodology flawed, and the generalizations they derived from unsystematic observation, however apt and based on experience, not demonstrably universal. The second type of theory carries out its pedagogic function by helping people think about war, not by offering them the finality of rules for action, but by outlining fundamental processes, such as moving from means to ends, and posing questions. Cognitive theory is related to the second type but goes further: it aims to develop an analytic representation of war by nonutilitarian study, concerned solely with gaining a deeper understanding of the subject. That understanding makes general propositions possible. Such an analysis might also lead to better performance, but that is not its immediate purpose, and its arguments are not directly oriented on success. In short, Clausewitz rejects didactic theory because rules prevent people from thinking on their own, freely, and because rules can never adequately reflect the range of unique military-political events. As I note below, he is willing to admit that rules apply to technical details and procedures, but

THE CONQUEST OF REALITY

otherwise only in the most general and tentative way. Rather than develop rules, theory should depict war, its elements and their manner of functioning, in a structural analysis as accurately as possible, so as to help an independent mind reach its own conclusions.

In view of these opinions, it cannot surprise that in the "Author's Preface" to *On War* Clausewitz declares he does not intend to be didactic or prescriptive. But how he makes this point is, to say the least, unusual in the history of military theory. He shows his impatience with system-makers by resurrecting a jest by Georg Friedrich Lichtenberg, professor of physics at the University of Göttingen and a famous satirist of the German Enlightenment. Not incidentally, a century later Lichtenberg's name occurs in the exchange of letters between Einstein and Freud, published under the title *Why War?*[30] As an example of the—to Clausewitz—absurd wish to formulate and observe rules for an activity he thinks is best carried out by the "creative spirit," he cites Lichtenberg's "Extract from a Fire Regulation."[31] It begins: "If a house is on fire, one must above all seek to save the right wall of the house on the left, and on the other hand the left wall of the house on the right. For if, for example, one were to . . . protect the left wall of the house on the left, one must remember that the right wall of the house is on the right of its left wall . . . and thus closer to the fire than the left," and so on for another dozen lines, all repeated by Clausewitz, until he has driven the belief in firm rules for such activities as war well and truly into the ground.

In *On War* Clausewitz turns his dissatisfaction with contemporary military theory into a program. "Our aim," he writes in the chapter on "Types of Resistance," "is not to provide new principles and methods of conducting war; rather, we are concerned with examining the essential content of what has long existed, and to trace it back to its basic elements."[32] It is worth noting the relationship of these words with the "Author's Preface" of 1816–1918. Another, more extensive rejection appears in the chapter "On the Theory of War," a text too often marginalized in the pragmatically oriented Anglo-American literature on Clausewitz. Tracing the history of military theory, Clausewitz writes: "Efforts were . . . made to equip the conduct of war with principles, rules, or even systems . . . [but] the conduct of war branches out in almost all directions and has no definite limits, while any system, any model, has the finite nature of a synthesis. An irreconcilable conflict exists between this type of theory and actual practice."[33] Instead, the tripartite nature of war must be recognized, not only pragmatically but in theory, which, he writes in the section headed "Theory Should Be Study, Not Doctrine," need not be

> a positive doctrine, a sort of *manual* for action. . . .
> Theory will have fulfilled its main task when it is used
> to analyze the constituent elements of war, to distinguish precisely what at first sight seems fused, to explain in full the properties of the means employed and
> to show their probable effects, to define clearly the

nature of the ends in view, and to illuminate all phases of warfare. . . . [Theory] is meant to educate the mind of the future commander, or, more accurately, to guide him in his self-education, not to accompany him to the battlefield; just as a wise teacher guides and stimulates a young man's intellectual development, but is careful not to lead him by the hand for the rest of his life.[34]

Believers in prescriptive analyses of war may object that these and similar expressions of Clausewitz's intentions should not be taken literally but are evocations of an ideal he cannot achieve. History becomes a simple matter when, without any supporting evidence, statements are dismissed as not being meant seriously. The simplifiers overlook the fact that not only does Clausewitz not offer rules, his theories may apply to any kind of campaign, any kind of war. He analyzes the nature of a major issue as best he can; the rest is up to the reader. An example of this detachment is his argument that as a logical consequence of the political nature of war, the political and military leaders should be in close communication, even interaction. But he never declares that in conducting war one type of political leadership or government is more effective than another.

◼ 4 ◼

Since Clausewitz and Jomini express clearly and often what they are about, how do so few comparisons of their ideas fully recognize their different intentions? The failing is so common that it deserves analysis. To review their positions: In his "Summary," Jomini states that he offers the reader "fundamental, immutable principles." His "consistently held intentions," to use John Shy's formulation, are "to reduce the complexity of warfare to the smallest number of crucial factors and to prescribe those lines of action that make victory most likely."[35] The subject of his work is the successful pursuit of war. Jomini, we might say, writes about warfare rather than war. Clausewitz, on the contrary, writes to explain war, shaped by society and politics, as it functions according to means and ends. Each component of war contains a universal, general core, a regulative idea, but is too singular, besides existing in a context of chance, uncertainty, and friction, to be subject to more than very general advice, which Clausewitz sometimes—as in the example of civil–military interaction—but not always offers. By studying particular phenomena, he comes to recognize the general characteristics of war, which in turn leads to a better understanding of the particulars.

If this obvious distinction between the two theorists is often ignored, then presumably it is because pragmatic interests dominate the study of war. Put differently, for most people the problems posed by war have always been a matter, first, of survival, and second, of victory. It is only natural that soldiers and politicians tend to think about war and perhaps read what is written about it, to help them succeed in war. Pragmatic concerns may also drive people to read *On War*, and when they do they may expect not only instruction but also the principles and laws of a dogmatic system. It is then hardly surprising that Clausewitz's statements of purpose are overlooked or dismissed as outdated "philosophical" musings, and he is read as though he were a needlessly complex, less straight-talking Jomini. One may of course argue that the best path to military success is to understand war in Clausewitz's sense: recognize the elements of war, their interaction in an uncertain environment within one belligerent and between opposing forces, the relationship of the strategic goal to the political end, and so on. Yet that is asking for too much. Understanding can exist on theoretical and on practical levels. Not everyone is concerned with ultimate truths, nor need be: throughout history, commanders whose instinct and practical sense outweighed their knowledge have achieved great things. But it is certain that readers who approach an analytic text like *On War* as a manual will stumble. Since pragmatism is ensconced in the study of war, many may find it difficult even to identify the problem, let alone follow Clausewitz in the detached abstractions of his reasoning.[36]

We must also recognize that some characteristics of *On War* encourage misconceptions. Clausewitz's attempt to understand war is facilitated by his effort to make his analysis as concrete as he can. His text includes dozens of historical examples, hundreds of historical references, to which he often adds his judgment on the appropriateness of the measures taken. Time-specific references come to support timeless recognitions. They respond to his effort to develop his ideas as near historical reality as he can, and they help us to understand him. But his use of examples also presents a danger. Readers—especially when they would welcome or expect rules—may easily take references that include the author's approval or criticism as positive instruction.

Clausewitz neither excludes all personal judgments from his historical references nor eliminates every didactic comment and remark from his text. These comments are never central, but they disturb the clarity of his approach. Perhaps his intended revision of the manuscript would have removed such inconsistencies. They do not change the nondidactic thrust of his work nor cancel his repeated declarations that he is writing an analytic, not a prescriptive, work. Still, as he left it, *On War* contains contradictions, not in his ideas but in their presentation, which may mislead readers.

Some readers may also find it difficult to accept that such a determined opponent of Napoleon could write a detached analysis of a subject in which Napoleonic war looms so large. Both before and after 1806, Clausewitz rejected Prussia's submission to the French order in Europe; in 1812 he quit the army so as not to serve Napoleon in his attack on Russia, an act that made him permanently suspect to his monarch. Surely objectivity could not be expected from such a man. On the contrary, even as he condemned Napoleon's character and policies, Clausewitz never ceased to praise him as the great commander, the genius who is above all rules! The need Clausewitz felt since youth to understand the condition of war-in-permanence in which he existed grew only stronger with time, however powerful his dedication to Napoleon's defeat. The search for objectivity that ruled his theoretical work also affected his life. During the years of reform, he was already shaking off the strict obedience to the state in which he had grown up; after 1815 his independence of mind made him suspect and isolated in the conservative resurgence in Prussia.

We see that there are many reasons why his theoretical work is open to misunderstanding, and it may be interesting to trace the genesis of one or the other of these errors. Here are two case studies from the years just before the First World War, the offenders Prussian officers, whose military education since adolescence included immersion in *On War.* A segment of German military opinion had always been troubled by Clausewitz's proposition that defense is the stronger form of war with the negative purpose; attack, the weaker form with the positive purpose. The idea was often rejected, but apparently not with sufficient finality, for in 1911 Friedrich von Bernhardi, a retired senior general, published an essay, "Clausewitz on Attack and Defense. Attempt at a Refutation."[37]

Bernhardi's article is one of several theoretical underpinnings for a book he was writing, *Germany and the Next War,* which called for Germany's further expansion to "true world power." The book's publication in 1912 turned out to be "a literary success and [for Germany] a political misfortune."[38] Translated into several languages, it was widely read as a proclamation of German imperial ambitions by an author who seemed to know a good deal about the inner workings of army and government, an impression that William II's stiff censure of the author and his book could only confirm. In his article, Bernhardi dismissed Clausewitz's argument that the defensive draws important advantages from its intimate knowledge of its own land and the support of its own people (which, incidentally, again reflects the power 1806 and other Napoleonic invasions exerted on Clausewitz's thought), by pointing out that Clausewitz's exclusive association of attack with invasion, and defense with one's own country, was erroneous. Defensive war, Bernhardi wrote, could also be waged in the enemy's country, where these advantages would not obtain—an observation soon borne out by German defensive operations in France in the First World War after the execution of Schlieffen's great enveloping offensive had failed. Bernhardi continued by arguing that Frederick the Great, "like all great commanders," believed the offensive to be superior to the defensive, and, revealing the purpose of his article, concluded that Frederick's opinion should also be that of Germans today: the offensive "alone suits a state, which like Germany is surrounded by enemies, and which would be ruined if it regarded the defense the stronger form of warfare."[39]

What Bernhardi does here is to transmute Clausewitz's analysis of defense and attack into strategic advice. But for Clausewitz to describe the defensive as innately stronger is not to propose that all wars should be fought defensively. The relative strength of different strategies is one issue to weigh among many. In Bernhardi's "Refutation," Clausewitz's attempt to understand two basic actions in war becomes a avoid major crises and decisive actions. . . . If his assumptions are sound and promise success we are not entitled to criticize him." But, Clausewitz adds, he must never forget that the enemy may be able to expand limited war to its logical absolute.[42]

In his urge to claim Clausewitz as an advocate of massive offensive, even total war, Schwertfeger passes over his statement that political aims and military conditions may call for means other than annihilation. He misunderstands the classical allusion, "the first-born son of war," Clausewitz's rather fanciful reference to his opening definition that war is theoretically not subject to any limitation of force, although in real life the use of maximum force (the "first-born son of war") may be modified by politics and other factors.

Both writers shorten Clausewitz's dialectical treatment of the polarities in war—absolute and real war, the dual nature of war, escalation but also modification of force, emotional and rational conduct of war—into unitary statements to match the critic's preference. Clausewitz and his two interpreters are driven by different motives: understanding, on the one hand; advocacy, on the other.[43]

⊠ 5 ⊠

In Schwertfeger's and Bernhardi's analyses of Clausewitz and their interpretation of Frederick the Great's wars, history and theory meet, as they do in Schlieffen's studies of the war of 1806, which were written in the same years.[44] These encounters raise general questions about the historical study of war, and it may be useful to look at some of the issues briefly before returning to the discussion of Clausewitz's theories.

Like all military defeats, the campaign of 1806 left the defeated with the question of why they had lost. That the French had an exceptionally gifted commander was a fortuitous reason; other reasons were intrinsic to the postrevolutionary French armies, and thus subject to analyses aiming at institutional reform. French operational and tactical superiority derived in part from developments within the army, but also from social and political change, which meant that contemporaries could understand the war and its outcome only by extending their analysis beyond the purely military. That holds equally true for historians who later would study the events of 1806. Since military and nonmilitary considerations interact in every war, a purely military analysis of an extended episode such as a campaign, either contemporary to the events or afterwards, can never ask all the questions and can never reach more than partial conclusions. Schlieffen, Bernhardi, and Schwertfeger, as we have seen, interpret the past from an exclusively military point of view. That perspective has great strengths, but, unaccompanied by other points of view, it prevented its practitioners from recognizing deeper causes, which in the end could weigh more heavily than the overt operational and tactical factors they analyzed with such knowledge and understanding.

But is it really the case that their analyses are limited to military issues? Yes, if we ignore their motives and concentrate on their writings. In their texts they insist on basing themselves on their familiarity with contemporary and past military institutions, and with the realities of war; but what they discuss and how they discuss it are determined by a host of nonmilitary motives and interests. Their analyses are in part generated, in part hobbled by political and social considerations, and no amount of technical insights can prevent their conclusions from being skewed. They are military specialists, but they combine their expert knowledge with partisanship.

Partisanship and preconceptions, however, know no boundary. In that respect the three German officers, whose interpretations of segments of their country's military past we have noted, may stand for all historians. We have all seen how extraneous concerns can stimulate and energize an interpretation, even as they positively or negatively affect insight and almost inevitably interfere with objectivity. Special pleading threatens accuracy, a threat historians know and are free to exclude from their work. But perhaps even more complex than joining one's expertise to special interests are the issues raised by combining expertise with different disciplines or subdisciplines in the study of war. That comprehensiveness reflects reality is a strong argument for interdisciplinary work. On the other hand, no historical interpretation can ever be complete, and that the past is multidimensional does not mean that its interpretation must be many-faceted. The past is sufficiently complicated to occupy any number of specialists, and an interdisciplinary approach to war is not the only one that is defensible and rewarding. Yet it does at least seem desirable for specialists to and when we reach the core of his thinking we are inevitably taken back to the ideas and the arts of his time and class: to the elevation of rationality, but also to the new recognition that the Enlightenment's near-religious faith in the rational put too heavy a burden on it, and to a new realization of the power of individual phenomena in place of former universal concepts, however impressive these had been intellectually and ethically. The new methods of critical analysis, which recognized the limitations of any theoretical system and saw that the irrational and other imponderables impose limits on ideas and actions—even as they expand them—shaped the young Clausewitz's thoughts on war. He adopted the techniques of critical analysis, its dialectic, and such concepts as polarity. His association with literature and the arts extended even to their theories, and his intellectual armory derives in part from late-eighteenth-century aesthetics.

At that time, the dividing line between science, scholarship, and the arts was not yet sharply drawn. German classicism valued and pursued the links between them. Schiller wrote a thesis on physiology and for years was known as much for his historical writings as for his poetry; Goethe published a study on the metamorphosis of plants and devoted much time to the theory of color. Lichtenberg discovered electrostatic figures, the so-called Lichtenberg Figures, and besides his satirical works also wrote hundreds of pages on the engravings of Hogarth, whose most important contemporary interpreter he became. The French Revolution had already run its course when Schiller and Goethe, who were not alone in thinking of the arts and the sciences as related approaches to truth, defined the relationship of the two in an epigram, one of their so-called tame gifts to German culture, little bombs to shake up people and stir debate. They gave it the title "Scientific Genius":

> Only the poet is born? No, the philosopher, too, is
>   born rather than made;
> In the end, the created truth is the only truth we can
>   see.[45]

It is not surprising then, though telling about his theories, that the young Clausewitz wrote several essays in which he clarified to himself what the applied arts, which include the art of war, could learn from theory in the fine arts.[46] We can identify one source for these borrowings: a course of lectures on Kant by Johann Gottfried Kiesewetter, which Clausewitz heard in Berlin in 1804 or 1805.[47] "Art," Clausewitz writes in one essay, "is trained ability." By clarifying the interaction of means and end, theory helps the artist to understand his work but does not show him how to do it. Clausewitz then distinguishes between principles and rules and moves from art to war: "Rules exist for the minutiae of service, for telling us how to set up camp or leave it, how to construct entrenchments, etc. But there are no rules for conducting a campaign or fighting a battle."[48] Significant results come from personal aptitude and free will—twenty years later he would have written, "come from the creative spirit." Opinion may differ on how much weight these borrowings from aesthetic theory should be given, but they clearly show Clausewitz reaching beyond the limits of the army and its institutions to the culture of his time and society as he begins to create his structural analysis of war.

This analysis has its limits, and not only because Clausewitz's early death kept him from completing his planned revisions of *On War*. If in many respects he was strengthened by the culture of his time, in others it let him down—the state of psychology in the late eighteenth century, for instance, left him ill equipped to address one of the issues dearest to him: the emotions of leaders and followers. Another possible gap is the matter of ethics in war, which, barring a few comments, Clausewitz excludes from his analysis, regarding it as part of society, its standards and its politics, not strictly speaking of war itself. Still, he might have discussed ethics, for instance in connection with his explorations of morale and discipline. It is a matter of defining the subject, and Clausewitz could have been right in excluding ethics, even if some of his readers today would regard the work as incomplete in this respect. Nevertheless, *On War* continues to interest many readers as containing ideas and discussions that are still valid, or at least deserve serious attention. Clausewitz retains a presence in today's thinking about war—surely more than Montesquieu, one of his intellectual models, retains in the discussion of the separation of powers in government, or even Adam Smith in modern economic theory. That we continue to turn to Clausewitz appears, however, to be at least as much in response to our dangerous world as from admiration of his work. Or perhaps it is merely a sign that some of his insights have become part of our intellectual vocabulary—however we use his concepts and arguments.

Even if today's concerns motivate our interest in his ideas, it may be advisable to see Clausewitz above all as a man of his time writing for his time. The still growing literature on the present relevance of his ideas too often treats him as our contemporary. That seems odd. Do we still cite Wilhelm von Humboldt or Thomas Arnold as though they were writing on university governance today? I hope we do; but only if we try to understand Humboldt, Arnold, and with them Clausewitz, in the context of their times, and if we do so as empathetic travelers in a foreign land, who in their judgments are able to rise above their own place- and time-bound ways.

Seen from a perspective centered on Clausewitz rather than on contemporary problems of national and international security, we recognize him as an unusually searching observer of a new phase of European and soon world history. Early on he began to track the back and forth of war and society in the changes that were occurring, and compared them with what had gone before. In the wars of his time and of the past, going back to tribes and nomads, he found elements that enabled him to see beyond the present to construct an image of war as such, which to a remarkable degree seems to incorporate recognitions that retain validity over long periods of time. In his response to the new, he is one of the strong voices of his generation. He may not say everything that we today believe needs saying—even the highest achievements of the creative mind reach forward to the work of others, who in their own way will add to it. But he is worth hearing—for his formulations and manner of arguing; for demonstrating that a structural analysis of war, the indispensable first step toward its mastery, is possible; and not least for exemplifying in his theoretical and historical work how far we can free ourselves from the restraints of the customary and accepted in thinking about one of the still prevalent realities of the human condition.

Notes

CHAPTER I: TWO BATTLES

1. Carl von Clausewitz, *On War*, transl. Michael Howard and Peter Paret (Princeton, 1976), 8, ch. 3, p. 593.

2. It could be interesting to examine how many of Clausewitz's contemporaries reached his conclusion that every future war might well be waged with "the full resources of the state," and what they meant by that. The expansion of war and the likely continuation of this process are repeatedly discussed in the nineteenth-century scholarly and military literature. A more recent example is David Bell's *The First Total War* (Baltimore, 2008), which interprets the wars of the revolution and of Napoleon as forerunners of the "total wars" of a later time. Bell seems unaware of the long and rich history of this thesis, and he does not sufficiently differentiate rhetoric and reality, policy and practice during the revolution and the First Empire. Nor, despite the intensification of warfare, was every war in the twentieth century "total."

3. Napoleon to Frederick William III, October 12, 1806, *Correspondance de Napoléon I* (Paris, 1863), 13:344.

4. E.g., Napoleon to Berthier, September 30, 1806, ibid., p. 284.

5. Note, for example, Bülow's statement, "Skirmishing is most in accord with the new way of war," in *Geist des neuern Kriegsystems* (originally published in 1799), reprinted in *Militärische und vermischte Schriften von Heinrich von Bülow*, ed. Eduard Bülow and Wilhelm Rüstow (Leipzig, 1853), p. 285.

6. The literature on 1806 is filled with widely conflicting figures for French and Prussian military strengths. Even at the time the men in charge were not always certain of the strengths of their commands. On September 30 Napoleon writes to his brother Louis that he will unite about 200,000 men on the battlefield, which was certainly between 15 and 20 percent too high, *Correspondance*, 13, p. 293. For strength and casualty figures, I base myself on such French and German archival studies as P. J. Foucart, *Campagne de Prusse (1806) Jéna* (Paris, 1887); and Oscar von Lettow-Vorbeck, *Der Krieg von 1806 und 1807*, 1 (Berlin, 1891), which are generally in agreement.

7. Napoleon to Berthier, September 30, 1806, *Correspondance*, 13, p. 285.

8. George Wilhelm Friedrich Hegel to Friedrich Immanuel Niethammer, October 13, 1806, *Briefe von und an Hegel*, ed. Johannes Hoffmeister (Hamburg, 1952), 1:120.

9. Johannes von Borcke, *Kriegerleben des Johannes von Borcke*, ed. v. Leszczynski (Berlin, 1888), p. 27.

10. Carl von Clausewitz, *Nachrichten über Preussen in seiner grossen Katastrophe*, Kriegsgeschichtliche Einzelschriften, no. 10, ed. Section for Military History, Great General Staff (Berlin, 1888), p. 435.

11. F. N. Maude, *The Jena Campaign, 1806* (London, 1909), p. 156.

12. *Rangliste der Königlich Preussischen Armee . . . 1806* (Berlin, 1806), pp. 136–38; Curt Jany, *Geschichte der Preussischen Armee*, 2nd rev. ed. (Osnabrück, 1967), 3:568.

13. Georg Wilhelm Friedrich Hegel to Friedrich Immanuel Niethammer, October 24, 1806, *Briefe von und an Hegel*, 1, 126. Johann Wolfgang von Goethe, Entry of October 14, 1806, *Tagebücher*, ed. Herbert Nette (Düsseldorf-Cologne, 1957), p. 83.

14. On Clausewitz's actions at the Battle of Auerstedt, see Lettow-Vorbeck, *Der Krieg von 1806 und 1807*, 1:392; and my *Clausewitz and the State*, 3rd rev. ed. (Princeton, 2007), p. 125.

15. According to the 5th Bulletin of the *Grande Armée*, Prussian losses in both battles were more than 20,000 killed and wounded, and between 30,000 to 40,000 prisoners; also captured were 25 to 30 flags and 300 cannon. An estimate of French losses was mini-

mized at 1,000 or 1,100 killed, and 3,000 wounded. *Bulletins de la Grande Armée* (Berlin, 1806) [published in the Royal Printing Plant after the French occupied Berlin], pp. 23, 25.

16. That was also Clausewitz's judgment. See *On War*, book 6, ch. 28, p. 494.

17. I give examples in my *Yorck and the Era of Prussian Reform, 1807–1815* (Princeton, 1966), pp. 209–13.

18. Alfred von Schlieffen, "Jena," in *Gesammelte Schriften* (Berlin, 1913), 2:214. Similar judgments may still be found in the modern literature. For a recent example, see Charles Esdaille, *Napoleon's Wars: An International History, 1803–1815* (New York, 2007), a work that, to be sure, concentrates not on strategy, operations, and tactics, but primarily on the interaction of politics, diplomacy, and war. On p. 270 the author refers to "the supposed inferiority" of Prussian tactics at Jena, a dismissive judgment that fails to explain the opinions of many soldiers at the time and ignores the obviously greater mobility and versatility of the French infantry, as well as the restrictive impact that Prussian organization, discipline, and supply had on the troops' manner of fighting.

19. Schlieffen, "Jena," p. 211.

CHAPTER 2: VIOLENCE IN WORDS AND IMAGES

1. I have discussed this subject in *Art as History* (Princeton, 1988), and in *Imagined Battles: Reflections of War in European Art* (Chapel Hill, 1997). Wolf Kittler's interesting monograph *Die Kultur des Partisanen aus dem Geist der Poesie: Heinrich von Kleist und die Strategie der Befreiungskriege* (Freiburg i. B., 1987) traces connections between the literature and the political and strategic decisions of this period but, as the title of his work suggests, argues for direct causal links between them, which seems to me not substantiated by the facts. Cultural phenomena reflect ideas and attitudes and help shape them, but it is not often that they serve as the principal and immediate triggers of decisions and action. More informative and realistic on the links between literature and politics at the time is the excellent article by Roger Paulin, "1806/07—ein Krisenjahr der Frühromantik?" *Kleist Jahrbuch*, 1993.

2. Georg Wilhelm Friedrich Hegel, "Die Verfassung Deutschlands," *Werke* (Frankfurt am Main, 1986), 1:483.

3. Heinrich Heine, *Das Buch Legrand* (Berlin, 1914), p. 36.

4. The ballad was inspired by an early document of the Napoleonic legend, Béranger's chanson "Les Deux Grenadiers" (1814), with its refrain "Vieux grenadiers, suivons un vieux soldat," a work much inferior to Heine's poem.

5. Hegel, "Die Verfassung Deutschlands," 451.

6. The print was published separately and as an insert in the journal *Neue Feuerbrände* 3, no. 7–9 (1807), "Amsterdam & Cölln." As a protection against censorship, the true place of publication, either Leipzig or Berlin, was hidden.

7. My translation. J.C.L. Grieser, *Schaudervolle Rückerinnerung an die Schreckens-Scene, welche sich vom 13ten bis 15ten Oktober 1806 in Jena zugetragen*, 2nd exp. ed. (Jena, 1806), facsimile inserted in Paul Schreckenbach, *Der Zusammenbruch Preussens im Jahre 1806* (Jena, 1913).

8. I have earlier discussed this print in my study *Imagined Battles*, pp. 63–64.

9. *Neue Feuerbrände*, no volume number indicated, no. 7, "Amsterdam & Cölln," 1807. The engraving appeared on the cover of at least two other issues of the journal. A related incident, possibly the factual source behind the image, is reported in Curt Jany, *Geschichte der Preussischen Armee*, 3:586: two ensigns threw flags in the river, and one jumped in as well but was captured by the French.

10. An important exception in the revolutionary and Napoleonic campaigns are French artists, working for the Ministry of War but also other official agencies, who, basing themselves on topographical studies and records of the forces engaged, produced some of the best pictorial accounts of war before photography. Nothing equivalent came from Germany at the time, since the organizational will, which provided funds and access to the necessary documents, was lacking. On the work of such artists as Carle Vernet and Jean Duplessix-Bertaux, see my *Imagined Battles*, pp. 58–62.

11. Johann Wolfgang von Goethe to J. H. Meyer, June 6, 1797, *Goethes Briefe* (Hamburg, 1964), 2:274.

12. Friedrich von Schiller, Prologue, *Wallensteins Lager*, lines 94–97.

13. In the large literature on Schiller's trilogy, I am particularly indebted to Walter Hinderer's remarkable study, *Der Mensch in der Geschichte: Ein Versuch über Schillers Wallenstein* (Königstein/Ts., 1980).

14. *Die Piccolomini*, act 1, scene 4.

15. Carl von Clausewitz, *Schriften-Aufsätze-Studien-Briefe*, ed. Werner Hahlweg (Göttingen, 1966), 1:700.

16. Carl von Clausewitz, *Der Feldzug von 1812 in Russland, Hinterlassene Werke* (Berlin, 1835), 7:227.

17. See chapter 4, section 6, below.

18. On the nationalistic corruption of Schiller's work, see chapter 17, "Nationales Trauerspiel?" in the excellent study by Alfons Glück, *Schillers Wallenstein* (Munich, 1976).

19. The suggestion is Hans Joachim Kreutzer's, in his fine essay "Blumen und Hafer in der Mark. Fontane und Kleist," *Fontane Blätter* 86 (2008), p. 131.

20. I have suggested some more specific aspects of the relationship between Kleist and Clausewitz in "Kleist and Clausewitz: A Comparative Sketch," in *Festschrift für Eberhard Kessel*, ed. Manfred Schlenke (Munich, 1982).

21. Translations are my own.

22. Act 5, scene 10.

23. The assumption, occasionally voiced, that Kleist based his account of the Battle of Fehrbellin on the battles of Jena or Auerstedt is, however, mistaken. It seems that he combined accounts of the historic battle with Archduke Charles's inconclusive victory over Napoleon at Aspern (May 21–22, 1809), which he himself witnessed, and early accounts of which he read. Note the careful reconstruction of Kleist's text and his sources in Richard Samuel and Dorothea Coverlid's edition of the play (Berlin, 1964).

24. Friedrich Gundolf, *Heinrich von Kleist* (Berlin 1932), pp. 140–42. The work, originally published in 1922, has been unduly ignored in the more recent literature, although many of Gundolf's interpretations continue to be employed today.

25. For the following I base myself primarily on Helmut Börsch-Supan and Karl Wilhelm Jähnig, *Caspar David Friedrich*

(Munich, 1973); and Joseph Leo Koerner, *Caspar David Friedrich and the Subject of Landscape* (New Haven, 1990), two excellent studies, neither of which, however, devotes much attention to the painting discussed here.

26. Börsch-Supan and Jähnig, *Caspar David Friedrich*, p. 327.

27. On the basic issues, see my two essays, "Nationalism and the Sense of Military Obligation" (1970), and "Conscription and the End of the Ancien Régime in France and Prussia" (1981), both now in a volume of my collected essays on the history of war, *Understanding War: Essays on Clausewitz and the History of Military Power* (Princeton, 1992).

CHAPTER 3: RESPONSES AND REFORM

1. Carl von Clausewitz, "Historische Briefe über die grossen Kriegsereignisse im Oktober 1806," *Minerva* 1 and 2 (January, February, and April 1807).

2. Clausewitz, *Nachrichten über Preussen in seiner grossen Katastrophe, Kriegsgeschichtliche Einzelschriften*, no. 10.

3. "Der Feldzug von 1813 bis zum Waffenstillstand," *Hinterlassene Werke des Generals Carl von Clausewitz über Krieg und Kriegführung* (Berlin, 1835), 7:253–54.

4. August Wilhelm Neithardt von Gneisenau, "Freiheit der Rücken," *Der Volksfreund*, July 9, 1808, reprinted in Georg H. Pertz, *Das Leben des Feldmarschalls Grafen Neithardt von Gneisenau* (Berlin, 1864), 1:385–87.

5. Scharnhorst's background and early career are summarized in my *Clausewitz and the State*, pp. 56–77, which also lists some of the extensive biographical literature.

6. Scharnhorst to the Prussian intermediary Karl Ludwig von Le Coq, October 25, 1800, *Scharnhorsts Briefe*, ed. Karl Linnebach (Munich-Leipzig, 1914), 1:210. Le Coq, of French descent, had himself changed from the Saxon to the Prussian service. In the following years Scharnhorst was considered for a senior position in the Royal Military College in High Wycombe, and as late as 1809 and 1810 his appointment as inspector general of the Royal Military College was under discussion. See *Scharnhorsts Briefe an*

Friedrich von der Decken 1803–1813, ed. Joachim Niemeyer (Bonn, 1987), pp. 30–33.

7. On Scharnhorst and the Military Society, see Charles Edward White, *The Enlightened Soldier* (New York, 1989).

8. Gerhard von Scharnhorst, *Militärische Schriften*, ed. Colmar von der Goltz (Dresden, 1891). It characterizes Scharnhorst's attention to the specific, yet always in its larger context, that he states it as "an undoubted truth that French skirmishers decided most of the encounters in this war" not by themselves, but by adding a new flexibility to the army and giving it the ability to function effectively in a variety of circumstances.

9. The memorandum, submitted either in 1805 or 1806, is reprinted in Colmar von der Goltz, *Von Rossbach bis Jena und Auerstedt* (Berlin, 1906). The cited passage is on p. 545.

10. The classic, fundamentally important analysis of reform attempts before the defeat is Otto Hintze's essay "Preussische Reformbestrebungen vor 1806," now in Otto Hintze, *Geist und Epochen der Preussischen Geschichte, Gesammelte Abhandlungen*, 3, ed. Fritz Hartung (Leipzig, 1943). An English translation, "Prussian Reform Movements before 1806," is in *The Historical Essays of Otto Hintze*, ed. Felix Gilbert (Oxford 1975), pp. 54–87, with a short, valuable introduction by the editor.

11. A detailed documentary study of the investigation was edited by Curt Jany, *1806: Das Preussische Offizierskorps und die Untersuchungen der Kriegsereignisse*, a publication of the Section for Military History II of the Great General Staff (Berlin, 1906).

12. Ibid., pp. 104–5. See also Carl Hans Hermann, *Deutsche Militärgeschichte: Eine Einführung* (Frankfurt am Main, 1966), p. 154; and Hans Stübig, *Armee und Nation* (Frankfurt am Main, 1971), pp. 128–31. The figures and percentages in the three works differ somewhat, and Hermann does not take account of officers who were killed or died of wounds. But all agree that general officers suffered the highest percentage of men punished.

13. On the history of the commission with an emphasis on infantry tactics, see my *Yorck and the Era of Prussian Reform, 1807–1815*, pp. 117–90.

14. Ibid., p. 53.

15. I discuss the very mixed evidence of Yorck's political views in ibid., pp. 220–45.

16. Ibid., p. 181.

17. Curt Jany, *Geschichte der Preussischen Armee*, 3:436; Stübig, *Armee und Nation*, p. 34.

18. Manfred Messerschmidt, *Offiziere im Bild von Dokumenten aus drei Jahrhunderten* (Stuttgart, 1964), p. 59.

19. On the introduction of conscription in France and Prussia, see my essay "Nationalism and the Sense of Military Obligation" (1970), now in my collection of essays *Understanding War*; and "Conscription and the End of the Old Regime in France and Prussia," *Geschichte als Aufgabe: Festschrift für Otto Büsch*, ed. Wilhelm Treue (Berlin, 1988).

20. Ludwig von Vincke to Stein, September 30, 1808, *Die Reorganisation des Preussischen Staates unter Stein und Hardenberg*, part II, ed. Rudolf Vaupel (Leipzig, 1938), 1:598–601.

21. See the interesting section "Der Landsturm als organisatorische Form des Volksaufstandes im Jahr 1813," in Reinhard Höhn, *Revolution—Heer—Kriegsbild* (Berlin, 1944), pp. 642–56.

22. The overwhelming evidence that Prussian strategic planning and operations never considered insurrection as more than a subsidiary seems to me to disprove Kittel's central argument (see ch. 2, n. 1, above).

23. Jany, *Geschichte der Königlich Preussischen Armee* (Berlin, 1933), 4:78.

24. Karl Demeter, *Das deutsche Offizierskorps in Gesellschaft und Staat 1650–1945* (Frankfurt am Main, 1965), pp. 4–5.

25. Regulation of August 8, 1808, in Messerschmidt, *Offiziere im Bild von Dokumenten aus drei Jahrhunderten*, pp. 171–73.

CHAPTER 4: THE CONQUEST OF REALITY BY THEORY

1. See, for instance, Daniel Reichel's essay "Jomini, ein Anti-Clausewitz?" in *Clausewitz, Jomini, Erzherzog Carl*, ed. Manfred Rauchensteiner (Vienna, 1988).

2. The best brief analysis of Jomini's life, writings, and influence is John Shy's essay, "Jomini," in *Makers of Modern Strategy*, ed.
Peter Paret (Princeton, 1986). Shy is criticized by Jean-Jacques
Langendorf in his encyclopedic, but at times very partisan, two-
volume work *Faire la guerre: Antoine-Henri Jomini* (Chêne-Bourg &
Geneva, 2002, 2004), 1:361–62. For help with Jomini's exceedingly
complicated bibliography, I am indebted to *Antoine-Henri Jomini:
A Bibliographical Survey* (West Point, N.Y., 1975), by my former stu-
dent John I. Alger, and to Eman M. Vovsi's unpublished Univer-
sity of Florida M.A. thesis, "Historian and Napoleon's General:
Antoine-Henri Baron de Jomini," Tallahassee, 2007.

3. On Clausewitz's family background and early history, see
my *Clausewitz and the State*, chs. 1–3.

4. Günther Gieraths, *Die Kampfhandlungen der Brandenburgisch-
Preussischen Armee, 1626–1807* (Berlin, 1964), pp. 111–13. In his comparison of the lives of Jomini and Clausewitz, Langendorf, *Faire la
guerre*, 1:331–32, does not note the differences in their experience
of combat.

5. The literature on Bülow is extensive. See, among others,
the introductory essays in *Militärische und vermischte Schriften von
Heinrich von Bülow* (Leipzig, 1853), by the two editors E. Bülow
and W. Rüstow; Robert R. Palmer's chapter "Frederick the Great,
Guibert, Bülow: From Dynastic to National War," in *Makers of
Modern Strategy*, ed. Edward M. Earle (Princeton, 1961); and my discussion in *Yorck*, pp. 80–82, and *Clausewitz*, especially pp. 90–94.

6. Personal communication from Eman M. Vovsi, who found
a French and a Russian copy, dated 1806, in the Moscow State
Library. It is interesting that a Russian text existed as early as 1806.
This edition is not listed in the works by Alger or Rapin, which
give 1807 as the date of the first publication.

7. Shy, "Jomini," p. 170.

8. Antoine-Henri Jomini, *Traité des grandes opérations militaires*,
4th augmented ed. (Paris, 1851), 3:333. Langendorf, *Faire la guerre*,
2:402, notes that Jomini would "later try to add depth to his work,
without ever putting the fundamental principles into question."

9. The formulation is John Shy's in "Jomini," p. 168.

10. The following is based on my discussion of Clausewitz's review "Bemerkungen über die reine und angewandte Strategie des Herrn von Bülow," *Neue Bellona* 9, no. 3 (1805), in "Clausewitz," in *Makers of Modern Strategy*, ed. Paret, pp. 189–91.

11. I have been criticized for stressing the continuity in Clausewitz's thought from his early writings to his last theoretical comments, a criticism grounded (1) in apparent unfamiliarity with Clausewitz's early writings, and (2) in the deeply pragmatic outlook that characterizes much of today's literature on Clausewitz, which emphasizes the conclusions of his arguments, not how he reached them or how they are placed and relate to each other in his structural analysis. Of course Clausewitz's ideas changed; often in a process of gradual evolution, now and then seemingly more abruptly—the remaining evidence does not always identify transitional stages. But from Clausewitz's earliest surviving notes a remarkable consistency is evident in his care for the logic, precision, and clarity in which he develops his arguments and defines his conclusions. His repeatedly expressed concern over method is central to his thought, which makes him a rarity among the writers on war of his time. A number of others—Hermann von Boyen comes to mind—were also interested in the methodologies of interpreting social reality, but the military literature was to the greatest extent pragmatic, oriented toward specific events, problems, and techniques.

Nor is it the case that important ideas of *On War* are not already present in Clausewitz's early writings, and I am not alone in having pointed this out. It is perhaps enough to refer to Eberhard Kessel, whose discovery and edition of Clausewitz's notes and essays on strategy, mostly written before 1806, Carl von Clausewitz, *Strategie* (Hamburg, 1937), is with Werner Hahlweg's editorial publications the most important contribution to Clausewitz literature of the past century. Referring to the argument of means and purpose, and of the destruction of the enemy's armed forces, Kessel writes that "We find the beginnings of this core element of the theory of war already in the Strategy of 1804" (p. 27). He continues that the argument is not fully developed, "but what already exists and reappears with minor modifications [in 1812] and in the work *On War*, is very characteristic and significant." Similar comments may be found on pp. 29 and 33, and Kessel concludes his introduction with the observation, "Strictly speaking the essential is already present, and the imperfections only increase the work's appeal. To speak with Ranke: 'We love youth and freshness, even when linked to some faults'" (p. 35). Note also Kessel's related essays, "Zur Genesis der modernen Kriegslehre. Die Entstehungsgeschichte von Clausewitz' Buch Vom Kriege," *Wehrwissenschaftliche Rundschau* III, 9 (1953), and "Die doppelte Art des Krieges", ibid., IV, 7 (1954). Surely it is not surprising that in the history of ideas, as in the history of literature, music, or art, early studies often contain thoughts and themes that reappear in the mature work fully developed and integrated in larger structures. Analyzed carefully, these early phenomena may contribute to our understanding of the work and of its creator. It does surprise on the other hand, when these hardly exceptional links between youth and maturity—whatever their significance—are simply denied.

12. Langendorf, *Faire la guerre*, 2:320–21.

13. Clausewitz, *Strategie*, p. 72.

14. "Über den Zustand der Theorie der Kriegskunst," undated early essay, published in Schering, ed., *Geist und Tat*, pp. 52–60.

15. Carl von Clausewitz, "Über Kunst und Kunsttheorie," in ibid., p. 154.

16. Carl von Clausewitz, "Author's Preface," in *On War*, ed. and transl. Michael Howard and Peter Paret (Princeton, 1976), p. 61. On the significance of this and other prefatory notes, see below.

17. Carl von Clausewitz, "Author's Comment," in ibid., p. 63.

18. Carl von Clausewitz, "Two Notes by the Author on His Plans for Revising *On War*—Note of 10 July 1827," in ibid., pp. 69–70.

19. Carl von Clausewitz, "Two Notes by the Author . . .—Unfinished Note. Presumably Written in 1830," in ibid., p. 70.

20. In his book *Decoding Clausewitz: A New Approach to On War* (Lawrence, Kans., 2008), Sumida severely criticizes Raymond Aron and me for believing that Clausewitz did not complete his

revisions, and that we therefore regard *On War* as unfinished in critical respects—never mind that I neither believe nor have ever asserted this. The uncertain evidence makes it possible to disagree on the extent of the revisions; but what matters above all is how far and in which way the assumption that not all intended revisions were carried out affects one's interpretation of the work as a whole. On that decisive point I regard the issue as spurious. Clausewitz himself states plainly that in his revisions he did not plan to change major concepts or arguments, but rather to reinforce already existing statements. Incomplete revisions of *On War* no more assure a flawed interpretation than completed revisions guarantee its opposite. It all depends on the interpreter. On that score Professor Sumida evokes little confidence. He criticizes me for arguing that Clausewitz tried to "explain the essential nature of war" (ibid., p. 59). On the contrary, he asserts, Clausewitz's "main theoretical concern . . . is the integrity of the processes of observation and analysis of past military events" (ibid.). If this distinction means anything, it is that Clausewitz is oriented toward the past and does not connect past and present, which is ludicrous. Anyone who has read Clausewitz on contemporary military events should know that in his mind past and present interact—surely not an uncommon condition—to create the strongest possible basis for analysis, whether of now or then. Clausewitz's theoretical work encompasses both, and it should not need pointing out that processes such as escalation or the interaction of war and politics remain in principle the same whether today or thousands of years ago.

Very likely, though we cannot be certain, the desire to analyze war came to Clausewitz from his need to understand what he experienced as an adolescent subaltern fighting in the Alsatian foothills. Complementing and enriching his experiences by studying the past presumably followed later. To compartmentalize and separate his wish to understand present and past, and each through the other, is an academic fantasy. It has no place either in Clausewitz's speculative thought or in his work.

21. Carl von Clausewitz to his bride Marie von Brühl, July 3, 1807, quoted in my *Clausewitz and the State*, p. 39.

22. See my introduction to part 1, "Historical Writings," in Carl von Clausewitz, *Historical and Political Writings*, ed. Peter Paret and Daniel Moran (Princeton, 1992).

23. The following benefits from the excellent summarizing discussion in Werner Hahlweg, *Carl von Clausewitz* (Göttingen, 1957), pp. 72–83. Hahlweg's modest biography and introduction to Clausewitz's work has been unduly overshadowed by his subsequent editions of and writings on Clausewitz. The little book has stood the test of time remarkably well, anticipates much later research, and adds to the debt every scholar of Clausewitz owes the author.

24. Clausewitz, *On War*, book I, ch. 1, pp. 75–89.

25. Ibid., book 6, ch. 26, p. 479.

26. Clausewitz, "Unfinished Note, Presumably Written In 1830," in ibid., p. 71.

27. Ibid.

28. "Note of 10 July 1827," in ibid., p. 69.

29. The following is based on my introductory essay, "The Genesis of *On War*," in Clausewitz, *On War*, p. 14.

30. The place of Lichtenberg in the dialogue is discussed in my essay "Einstein and Freud's Pamphlet *Why War?*" *Historically Speaking* 6, no. 6 (July–August 2005), pp. 16–17.

31. Clausewitz, "Authors Preface," in *On War*, pp. 61–62.

32. Ibid., book 6, ch. 8, p. 389. See also n. 16 above.

33. Ibid., book 2, ch. 2, pp. 134.

34. Ibid., p. 141.

35. Shy, "Jomini," p. 172.

36. I discuss this issue at greater length in "Anmerkungen zu Clausewitz," in *Denkwürdigkeiten der Politisch-Militärischen Gesellschaft*, no. 43 (February 2008).

37. Friedrich von Bernhardi, "Clausewitz über Angriff und Verteidigung. Versuch einer Widerlegung," Beiheft 12 to *Militär-Wochenblatt*, 1911.

38. Gerhard Ritter, *Staatskunst und Kriegshandwerk* (Munich, 1960), 2:142. Bernhardi's book was reprinted three times within a year after it first appeared.

39. Bernhardi, p. 412.

40. Bernhard Schwertfeger, "Die Strategie Friedrichs des Grossen im Siebenjährigen Krieg," reprinted in his *Kriegsgeschichte und Wehrpolitik* (Potsdam, 1938), pp. 28–29.

41. Ibid., pp. 32–33.

42. Ibid., n. p. 33. The quotation is from *On War*, book 1, ch. 2, p. 99.

43. An important exception to these misinterpretations is the work another senior German officer published in these years, Lieutenant General Richard von Caemmerer's *Clausewitz* (Berlin, 1905). Caemmerer defends Clausewitz's treatment of attack and defense (pp. 107–12). In connection with a discussion of Jomini's writings (pp. 95–96) he stresses Clausewitz's rejection of all strategic systems and rules.

44. See Schlieffen's discussion of the war of 1806 in chapter 1 above.

45. *Xenien*, no. 20: "Wird der Poet nur geboren? Der Philosoph wird's nicht minder; / Alle Wahrheit zuletzt wird nur gebildet, geschaut."

46. Clausewitz, "Über Kunst und Kunsttheorie" and "Über den Begriff des körperlich Schönen," in Schering's edition of Clausewitz's writings, *Geist und Tat* (see also notes 15 and 45 above).

47. On Kiesewetter, see my *Clausewitz and the State*, pp. 69, 75, etc. Note also Werner Hahlweg's concurring reference to my argument in his comments on the significance of Kiesewetter and aesthetic theory for the development of Clausewitz's ideas in his edition of Clausewitz's texts and letters, Carl von Clausewitz, *Schriften—Aufsätze—Studien—Briefe* (Göttingen, 1990), vol. 2, part 1, p. 19. Clausewitz was not the only soldier to explore aesthetic theory for other uses. Hahlweg, ibid., part 2, pp. 1211–15, prints parts of undated notes by Hermann von Boyen, Clausewitz's close associate during the reform era, a defender of the Landwehr, and future minister of war, which contain similarities to Clausewitz's notes on aesthetic theory and its application to war.

48. Clausewitz, "Über Kunst und Kunsttheorie," *Geist und Tat*, p. 162.

Index

Clausewitz, Carl von (*continued*)
characteristics of war, 123;
comparison with Jomini, 107–8,
121, 128–29; continuity and
change in his thought, 113,
154–55n11; criticism of Bülow,
113–14; criticism of Jomini, 115,
116; current interest in his work,
141–43; description of Rüchel,
23; on differing intensities in
war, 123, 124; dissatisfaction with
contemporary military theory,
127–28; early definition of
tactics and strategy, 114; on ends
and means in war, 122; exclusion of ethics from his work,
141; historical examples in *On
War*, 117, 130–31; "historicism"
of, 121; impact of literature,
philosophy, and aesthetic theory
on his thought, 54–55, 59, 106–7,
138–41; influence of Scharnhorst
on, 82; influences on his structural analysis of war, 55, 138–39;
interpretation of his theories by
other military authors, 132–35,
138; lectures on the "little" war
and guerrilla warfare, 97; major
topics of *On War*, 122–24; methodology a dominant issue in his
thought, 115–17; military career
of, 109–10; on motivations for
war, 122–23; and Napoleon,
131–32; on the nature and forms
of war, 122; as observer of European and world history, 142–43;
the "regulative idea" of war, 120,
121; rejection of didactic theory,
125–26; relation of theory to

reality in his thinking, 116–17,
123; resigns from the Prussian
service, 54–55; responses to
the Prussian defeat at Jena and
Auerstedt, 73–75; significance
of 1806 for the development of
his theoretical understanding of
war, 106–7; strategic thought of,
115–16; structural analysis of war,
55, 59, 119, 120, 122, 126, 139,
141, 143, 154n11; summary of the
reform era, 87–88; three types of
theory (prescriptive, pedagogic,
cognitive) delineated by, 125;
use of ideal concepts to measure
reality, 120; on waging war with
the full resources of the state,
145n2

Clausewitz, Marie von, 118
Coleridge, Samuel Taylor, 52, 53
Cölln, Friedrich von, 44–46
Convention of Paris, 76
Cross in the Mountains, The (Fried-
rich), 63

Das Buch Legrand (Heine), 37, 40
David, Jacques-Louis, 34–35
Davout, Louis-Nicolas, 17, 19, 21,
25, 26
Delbrück, Hans, 29
Disasters of War (Goya), 69
Droysen, Johann Gustav, 29
Dumouriez, Charles-François, 49

Engels, Friedrich, 29
Enlightenment, the, 36, 63, 77, 106,
126, 139
"Extract from a Fire Regulation"
(Lichtenberg), 126

Eylau, battle of, 83; paintings of, 69–70

Frederick II, King of Prussia, 6, 11, 61, 88, 90, 112, 121, 133, 134
Frederick William III, King of Prussia, 9, 10, 25, 26, 62, 77, 83–84, 85–86, 87, 100, 103
"Freedom for Backs" (Gneisenau), 78
French Revolution, 6, 16, 21, 38, 49, 68, 105, 139; influence on the Prussian military and bureaucratic elite, 77–78; influence on rank and file, 56, 73; *levée en masse* as a qualified political-military model for Prussian reforms, 95
Friedrich, Caspar David, 48, 67, 69, 71; pantheistic nature of his art, 63–64
Fussjäger, 15, 90

Geissler, Gottfried, 38–43, 69; engraving of the French entering Leipzig, 39–40, 148n6; engraving of the French entering Lübeck, 41–43
"General Reasons for the Successes of the French in the Revolutionary War, The" (Scharnhorst), 80–81
Gerby, Servan de, 105
Gneisenau, August Wilhelm Neidhardt von, 55, 78, 86, 100; defense of Kolberg by, 83
Goethe, Johann Wolfgang von, 16, 24–25; on Friedrich's paintings, 64; on Lessing's *Minna von Barnhelm*, 49; on Schiller's *Wallenstein*,

48–49, and Schiller on "Scientific Genius," 139–40
Goetzen, Friedrich Wilhelm von, 83, 86, 100
Goya, Francisco de, 69
Gros, Antoine-Jean, 69
Gundolf, Friedrich, 63, 149n24

Habermas, Jürgen, 35
Hahlweg, Werner, 154n11, 157n23, 158n47
Hannibal, 30
Hegel, Georg Wilhelm Friedrich, 21–22, 24, 25, 69, 138; characterization of Prussian government, 36, 38
Heine, Heinrich, 37, 38, 40
Hohenlohe, Friedrich Ludwig von, 20–21, 22, 27
Humboldt, Wilhelm von, 142

"In a Battle" (Schiller), 48
insurrection, 97–98, 152n22

Jena, 16, 17; looting of, 24, 40; panic among troops, 19. *See also* Jena, battle of
Jena, battle of, 22–25; casualties, 24; historical interpretation of, 27–28, 29–30
Jomini, Antoine-Henri, 8, 18, 105–6, 153n8; comparison with Clausewitz, 107–8, 113, 114–16, 121, 128–29; early writings of, 110; education of, 108; on the fundamental strategic principle of war, 112–13; military career, 108–9, 111–12; service under Marshal Ney, 111–12

between law and passion, and
war as metaphor of the human
condition, 63; treatment of politically sensitive matter, 61–62

Quintilius Varus, 57, 65

Radziwill Anton Heinrich, Prince,
62
*Résumé des principes généraux de
l'art de la guerre* (Jomini), 111–12,
153n6
Romanticism, 78
Rüchel, Ernst von, 20; fails to
reinforce Hohenlohe, 23–24;
wounded, 24
Rules and Regulations (British regulations), 92
Russia, 9, 11, 49, 57, 65, 100, 110,
112, 134

Saale River, strategic importance
of, 18–19
Saalfeld, engagement of, 18–19
Saving the Colors (1807), 44–45, 148n9
Saxony, Saxon army in war of 1806,
9, 16–17, 19
Scharnhorst, Gerhard von, 25,
84, 113, 150–51n6; actions at
Auerstedt, 82; actions at Eylau,
83; analysis of French successes
in the 1790s, 80–81; background
and early career, 79; commissioned in the Prussian service
and ennobled, 79–80; director of
the Military Society, 80; head of
the Academy for Young Infantry
and Cavalry Officers, 80; head
of the Military Reorganization

Commission (1807–1812), 84–88;
plans for the future structure of
the army, 97, 98–99; plans for opposing Napoleon, 97–98; success
and failure of, 102–3; technical
mastery of, 82
Schiller, Friedrich von, 47, 51, 52,
67, 69, 139–40; early career of, 48;
historical writings, 139; influence
on Clausewitz, 54–55; Schiller
and Goethe on "Scientific
Genius," 139–40; understanding
of war, 48–49, 53–54
Schlieffen, Alfred von, 135, 136, 138;
on the battle of Jena, 30–32
Schwertfeger, Bernhard, 136; interpretation of Clausewitz's *On War*,
134–35
Seven Years War (1756–1763), 11, 49,
100, 110, 112, 134
Silesia, defense of, 82–83
skirmishing, 24, 91–93, 110; as an
innovation of the "new" wars,
14–15, 145n5, 151n8
Soult, Nicolas Jean-de-Dieu, 17
Sumida, Jon Tetsuro, 119, 155–56n20
Swebach, Jacques François, 43

Tempelhof, Georg Friedrich von,
110
"Theory of the Art of War Today,
The" (Clausewitz), 116
Thirty Years War (1618–1648), 43,
48, 57, 76
Traité de grande tactique (Jomini), 111

Wallenstein, Albrecht von, 47, 48–49
Wallenstein's Camp (Schiller), 49–52,
70; the army main character of